学习策略与思维训练双融入1+X+Y 特色课程群优质教学设计案例研究

XUEXI CELÜE YU SIWEI XUNLIAN SHUANGRONGRU 1+X+Y
TESE KECHENGQUN YOUZHI JIAOXUE SHEJI ANLI YANJIU

周利君　向小婷　雷涵彧　编著

重庆大学出版社

内容提要

《学习策略与思维训练双融入 1+X+Y 特色课程群优质教学设计案例研究》一书旨在探讨高校如何将学习策略和思维训练融入到课程教学中,由理论探讨和案例分析两部分内容组成。本书基于"1+X+Y 特色课程群"的实践经历,在介绍其构建依据和理念的基础上,围绕学习策略和思维技能训练中的自我系统、元认知系统、认知系统和记忆系统从教学目标、教学手段、考核评价等方面,多维度论述了课程实现学习策略和思维训练"阶梯式"融入路径。同时,本书还选取了多门具体课程的优质教学设计案例,进一步呈现"双融入"的实践步骤和意义。

图书在版编目(CIP)数据

学习策略与思维训练双融入"1+X+Y"特色课程群优质教学设计案例研究:英文、汉文 / 周利君,向小婷,雷涵彧编著 . -- 重庆:重庆大学出版社,2020.12
ISBN 978-7-5689-2501-3

Ⅰ . ①学… Ⅱ . ①周… ②向… ③雷… Ⅲ . ①英语 – 教学设计 – 高等学校 Ⅳ . ① H319.3

中国版本图书馆 CIP 数据核字(2020)第 229767 号

学习策略与思维训练双融入 1+X+Y 特色课程群优质教学设计案例研究
周利君　向小婷　雷涵彧　编著

责任编辑:张晓琴　　版式设计:古万兰
责任校对:关德强　　责任印制:赵　晟
*
重庆大学出版社出版发行
出版人:饶帮华
社址:重庆市沙坪坝区大学城西路 21 号
邮编:401331
电话:(023)88617190　88617185(中小学)
传真:(023)88617186　88617166
网址:http://www.cqup.com.cn
邮箱:fxk@cqup.com.cn(营销中心)
全国新华书店经销
POD:重庆新生代彩印技术有限公司
*
开本:787mm×1092mm　1/16　印张:9.75　字数:278 千
2020 年 12 月第 1 版　2020 年 12 月第 1 次印刷
ISBN 978-7-5689-2501-3　定价:53.00 元

前　言

自 2012 年始，重庆第二师范学院外国语言文学学院在英语专业人才培养中开设《英语学习策略与思维训练》课程；2015 年，为加大学生语言能力与思维能力同步培养力度，特依托巴渝海外引智计划引进英国纽卡斯尔大学梅林博士，组建"融思促学"教学改革与研究团队，尝试在专业人才培养系列课程中开展思维训练教学改革与研究。

2017 年，团队针对国内高校普遍缺乏系统性学习策略和思维技能指导与训练这一难题，在借鉴和吸取国内兄弟院校实践经验的基础上，开始在英语（师范）专业人才培养中，从人才培养目标和毕业要求出发，以学习策略与思维训练指导与训练为切入点，根据课程性质和地位、课程关系和先后顺序，选取 1 课程（《英语学习策略与思维训练》）、X 语言类课程（《综合英语》《英语视听说》《英语读写》等）和 Y 其他类课程（《中国文化概论》《英语课堂教学综合实践》《学术论文写作》等），构建了学习策略与思维训练双融入"1+X+Y特色课程群"（以下简称为"1+X+Y课程群"）。

经过两年多的"1+X+Y课程群"建设与实践，团队发现思维能力培养要取得成效，必须走出传统教育重认知、轻实训的误区，除单独开设专门的思维课程外，还应该在各门课程中融入学习策略和思维技能的指导与训练。"1+X+Y课程群"规避了单独附加式思维教学的不足，灵活地发扬了嵌入式思维教学优点，实现了从"嵌入式"到"融入式"的整合，根据不同课程性质和不同阶段学习需求充分地体现了思维教学与课程教学的关系。

为总结"1+X+Y课程群"实践经历，团队编著此书，在介绍"1+X+Y课程群"构建依据和理念的基础上，与同行交流各代表课程在课程群中的定位与价值以及内容与任务，并以一个具体章节的若干教学设计为例进行设计理念和达成说明。

本书由周利君主持编写、统稿和审校，各部分编写分工具体如下：第一篇"1+X+Y特色课程体系"由周利君编写完成；第二篇"1 课程优质教学设计"由周利君、雷涵或编写完成；第三篇"X 课程优质教学设计"由马萍、左婷婷、向小婷编写完成；第四篇"Y 课程优质教学设计"由李佳、邹娟、周利君编写完成。

由于团队水平有限，难免错漏，敬请专家和同行批评指正。

编者
2020 年 7 月

CONTENTS
目 录

第一篇　1+X+Y 特色课程体系

第二篇　1 课程优质教学设计

第三篇　X 课程优质教学设计

第四篇　Y课程优质教学设计

1+X+Y 特色课程体系

伴随着课程改革的层层推进，学习者学习质量成为全球教育研究热点之一。大部分学生英语学习方法多为记忆、重复、复述，未能对学习内容进行自我构建，未能对学习过程进行监控与反思，学习方法不利于思维能力的培养与发展（周绵绵等，2011；张维友，2012；文秋芳，2012）。如何在学习过程中提供科学的指导与训练受到广大教育工作者和研究者的重点关注。高等学校人才培养过程中，如何构建有效的课程群和最大化课程群合力、提供系统有效的学习策略和思维技能指导与训练，值得深入探索。

第一部分
研究依据

一、理论依据

Bruner 等（1956）首次提出了"认知策略"的概念；Gagne（1977）认为，认知策略是学习者用来调节自己注意、学习、记忆和思维的内部过程，其功能在于使学习者不断反省自己的认知活动，不断调节与控制学习过程。Flavell（1979）最早提出了"元认知"的概念，他认为元认知就是对认知的认知，是个体对自己认知过程和结果的意识与控制，元认知包括元认知知识、元认知体验和元认知监控与调节三个方面，元认知监控和调节是其中关键。

20 世纪 80 年代以后，国内外兴起一股研究语言学习策略的热潮。不同研究者对学习策略的定义不同，就其是行为表现还是意识活动，存在争议。Oxford（1989）倾向于把学习策略定义为行为或行动，而 Weinstein 和 Mayer（1983）则认为学习策略既可以是行为，也可以是思想。Chamot（1999:2）认为，多数学习策略都是思维过程。

思维能力是人脑的高级认知能力，思维是"人脑对客观事物的本质和事物内在的规律性关系的概括与间接的反应"（朱智贤 & 林崇德，2002）。思维能力从属于认知能力，但在与语言相关的研究中，多数研究者将语言与思维相关联，或将思维与认知统一为思维（Dewey，1933；Whorf，1956；Vygotsky，1964；Udall & Daniels，1991；Tishman & Perkins，1997；Waters，2006）。

O'Malley 和 Chamot（1990）根据 Anderson（1983）的认知理论和信息加工理论将学习策略分为认知策略、元认知策略和社会情感策略，来源于实证研究，较为全面，具有一定的代表性，被许多同行借鉴和引用。

学习策略中的元认知策略和认知策略与思维训练紧密相关。元认知策略用于评价、管理、监控认知策略的使用，而认知策略是通过对学习材料直接分析、转化或综合来解决问题的步骤和活动。袁炳宏（2004）概括到："元认知策略主要是宏观上的调控,涉及学习计划、监控和评估;认知策略更多是微观层面上的操作,直接对具体的任务进行管理。"在学习活动中,认知策略是提高学习效率必不可少的具体策略性知识,而元认知则表现为对整个学习活动进行监控和调节。使用认知策略是为了取得进步,而使用元认知策略是为了监控学习进步的过程。社会情感策略设计了学习者与其他学习者和以英语为母语的说话者的交流或控制自我情感的方式,在听、说、读、写等各个方面均有所应用。（宋航,2007）

语言学习策略的使用是一个非常复杂的过程,任何一类策略都不是孤立使用的。完成一个语言活动至少会用到一类策略或是几类策略,而且在活动的不同阶段用到的策略也各不相同。由于学习者学习风格和学习活动性质的不同,哪些策略适用于哪个活动并没有现成的答案。

思维训练的目的是要提高受训者在认知过程中表现出的各种认知能力。而在认知过程中,认知策略与元认知策略共同作用,相互联系,相互作用,相辅相成。那么,思维训练既需要教授具体的认知策略,也不能忽视元认知能力的培养（杜晓新,1993）。认知策略又联结着不同的思维训练点,即具体的思维技能,能有效地将两者结合,则学习策略更有实效性,同时也能够提高心智操作能力,有益于思维能力的培养（关文信等,1998）。就认知策略来看,少数研究者明确罗列出其中所关联的思维技能,但并不完整,也未进行分类分级,较为散乱。

Cotterall S. 和 Reinders H.（2007）总结了学习策略融入课程教学主要有三种模式:集中式策略培训,即集中一段时间专门培训策略,如一个月、一个学期等,学习者可得到聚焦式专题培训,但可能会因为缺乏应用而不能迁移;融入式策略培训,即把培训渗透到日常教学中,学习者在不同的学习任务中有更多的机会应用和迁移;辅助式策略培训,即将策略培训放在学习任务后,通过反思策略的使用,提高策略意识,进而提高策略使用水平。

思维技能相对于思维能力理解难度系数低,以某种思维理论框架作为外语教学的依托,涵盖不同层级思维技能的训练,在教学中具有更强的实操性。Marzano 等（1988）在《Dimensions of Thinking》一书中,列出了八类 21 项核心思维技巧（core thinking skills）,指出它们均有文献和研究结果支持,是"学生必须学、学校必须教"的内容,肯定了思维技巧可经由教学予以强化。Waters（2006）结合外语教学的情境对布鲁姆的"教育目标分类"模型进行解读,认为语言教学中应包含不同层级思维能力的训练,如记忆能力、信息转换能力、信息解读能力、简单应用能力、分析能力、综合运用能力和评价能力。

国外研究者概括出了"为思考教学（Teaching for Thinking）""教思考方法（Teaching of Thinking）""教关于思考（Teaching about Thinking）""运用思考的教学（Teaching with Thinking）"等思维教学方法（杨思贤、李子健,2013）与"过程模式""内容模式"和"注入模式"三种思维教学模式（王帅,2011）,其中"注入模式"旨在融合思维训练教学和学科教学，学科的特殊性为思维技能提供了更富针对性的选择和运用，学科教学目标和思维能力发展更加清晰，受到普遍认可。

综上所述，学习策略与思维训练紧密相关，多数学习策略都是思维过程；思维训练旨在提高学习者在认知过程中所表现出的认知能力，认知过程中认知策略与元认知策略相互作用；融入式训练能提供更多的应用和迁移，双融入式训练能在认知过程中教授认知策略和元认知策略，同时发展认知能力和元认知能力。

二、实践依据

2003 年教育部正式启动的"高等学校教学质量和教学改革工程"明确提出要把新时代大学生培养成能够运用一定策略进行自主学习的学习者。基于国内缺乏专门的教材，潘亚玲（2004）、张维友（2004）、周绵绵（2011）等相继就英语学习策略与技能出版了国家规划教材和专著，供高等学校开设专门的课程，帮助学生了解学习策略的定义与分类、影响学习策略形成和使用的各种因素以及开展语言知识学习策略、语言技能发展策略培训等。截止目前，国内大多数高校采取在课程教学中融入学习策略指导，但因为缺乏系统的指导和长期的训练，指导质量欠佳；仅有少量的高校单独开设了英语学习策略与技能课程，但同样因为这种课程式的集中培训课时有限和缺乏课外应用，导致学生不能较好迁移、课程结束则意味着培训结束等问题。

近年来，一些大学开始尝试通过单独开设思维课程来培养大学生的思维能力。清华大学开设了"解决问题的策略与技能"选修课，北京航空航天大学开设了"大学学习指导"选修课；这些课程以学习解决问题的策略为中心，从培养学生的自我监控能力，学会如何思考入手，来提高其思维水平（江丕权、李越，2004）。北京大学和中国青年政治学院开设了"逻辑与批判性思维"通选课，围绕对论证的理解、分析、重构、评估展开，通过论证逻辑训练来提高学生的思维能力（谷振诣、刘壮虎，2006）。除尝试单独开设专门的思维课程外，国内也有少量在具体学科中培养学生思维能力的做法，王维利（2006）等和游坤（2007）等在护理专业教学中开设了思维与沟通课程；外语界的刘伟、郭海云（2006）、文秋芳（2009）、李荣华（2014）、陈钰（2016）、谢建伟（2016）等尝试在英语专业和非英语专业的阅读、写作、英语演讲等课程中培养学生的思维能力。

综合以上，思维能力培养要取得成效，必须走出传统教育重认知、轻实训的误区，除单独开设专门的思维课程外，还应该在各门课程中融入思维技能训练，全面促进学习者思维能力的提高和人格的完善。

第二部分
体系构建

重庆第二师范学院外国语言文学学院"外语教育学习策略与思维技能双融入"特色研究团队在国内外理论研究和实践探索的基础上，以英语（师范）专业人才培养课程体系改革为例，突破传统学习指导与思维培养模式及思路，选取代表性专业基础能力必修课和核心能力必修课，构建 1+X+Y 课程群，多维度改革"1 课程——语言类课程——其他类课程"课程群整体设计，实现学习策略与思维技能过程性梯级"双融入"，服务学生语言能力、思维能力、文化素养、职业能力、学术能力等的综合提升。

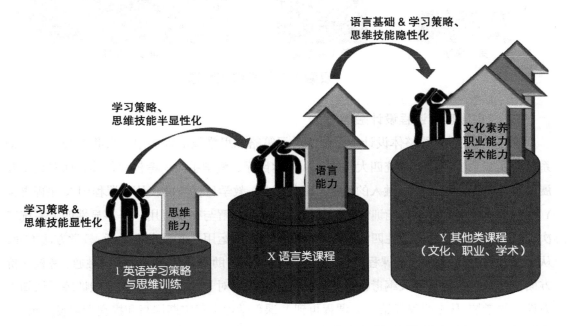

"双融入""阶梯式" 1 + X + Y 课程群构建模型

一、"双融入"代表课程精选

以《英语学习策略与思维训练》为 1 课程，选取《综合英语》《英语听说》和《英语读写》为 X 语言类课程代表，选取《中国文化概论》《英语课堂教学综合实践》和《学术论文写作》为 Y 其他类（文化类、职业类、学术类）课程代表，进一步彰显各代表课程现有的特色，凝聚学习策略和（或）思维技能训练合力，构建 1+X+Y 特色课程群。

1 课程《英语学习策略与思维训练》提供方法指导和实践应用，在第 1 学期开设，共 30 学时，理论学时和实训学时各占 50%；X 语言类课程服务学生语言能力提升，主要在第 1-4 学期开设；Y 其他（文化类、职业类、学术类）课程服务学生文化素养、职业能力和学术能力的提升，主要在第 5-7 学期开设。"双融入" 1+X+Y 特色课程群选取的课程在外语专业人才培养方案中具有较强的代表性，科学地分布在人才培养的整个过程中。

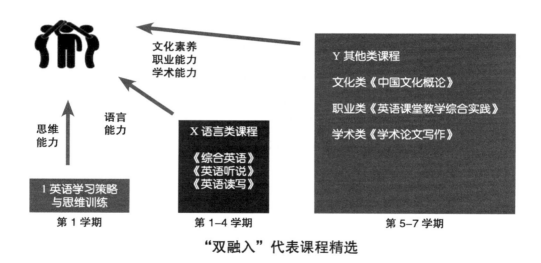

"双融入"代表课程精选

二、"多维度"课程设计融通

在 1+X+Y 课程群整体设计中，围绕学习策略和思维技能训练中的自我系统、元认知系统、认知系统和记忆系统四大系统，从教学目标、教学手段、考核评价等方面多维度开展改革，确保"阶梯式"融入的落地，具体包括：教学目标方面，从 1 课程到 X 课程再到 Y 课程学习策略与思维技能训练的"显性四大系统理解与初步运用——半显性四大系统二次理解与反复运用——隐性四大系统深度理解与灵活运用"，达成分层融通；教学方法方面，从 1 课程到 X 课程再到 Y 课程全程专业术语显性化辅助与强化，实现手段融通；考核评价方面，在原有课程教学大纲考核要求的基础上，增加对学习策略与思维技能训练元认知能力部分的考核，从 1 课程开始到 X 课程再到 Y 课程学生全程定期撰写和提交学习反思报告、任课教师定期撰写和提交教学反思报告，两类报告内容和质量计入学生课程考核中的"技能训练"部分，实现评价在课程体系中的全过程融通。

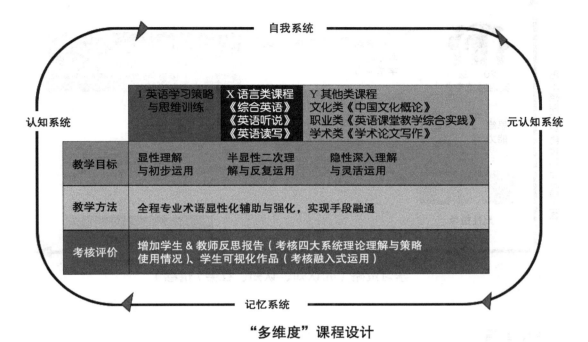

"多维度"课程设计

三、"阶梯式"融入路径实践

在 1+X+Y 课程群中分层次融入学习策略与思维技能训练，1 课程主要承担学习策略与思维技能的显性指导，基于自我系统、元认知系统、认知系统和记忆系统四大系统运作原理，以布鲁姆修订版教育目标分类框架为基础，结合具体的英语语言学习情境，训练学生在语言知识学习和语言技能发展中如何有效地应用学习策略、运用恰当的思维技能和思维工具；X 课程主要承担学习策略与思维技能的强化应用，训练学生在语言知识学习和语言技能发展中反复使用恰当的思维技能和思维工具，科学运用元认知策略、认知策略和社会情感策略助力学习质量的提升；Y 课程主要承担学习策略与思维技能的自主迁移，训练学生在文化、职业、学术等学科内容学习中自主运用恰当的思维技能和思维工具，科学运用元认知策略、认知策略和社会情感策略助力文化素养、职业能力和学术能力的提升。整体上在人才培养过程中全程阶梯式实践"显性指导 ——强化应用——自主迁移"的融入路径。

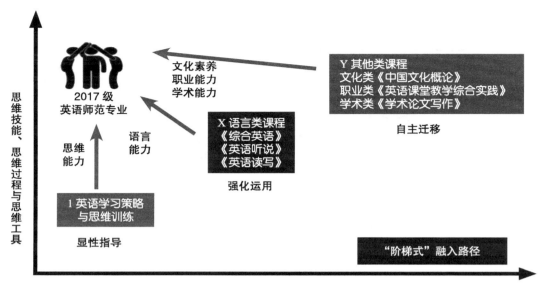

四、结语

1+X+Y 特色课程群的构建，打破了传统学习策略指导单一融入模式，在梯级系列课程中实行学习策略与思维技能指导与训练的双融入；突破了独立开设课程的课时与应用限制，强调英语学习策略与思维技能"显性化——半显性化——隐性化"梯级过程性双融入；走出了传统教育重认知、轻实践的误区，全面服务学生学习策略和思维技能指导与训练的质量提升，最终服务学生学习质量的提升。

截止目前，该特色课程群已经在 2017 级—2019 级英语（师范）专业人才培养中开展了为期 2 年多的实践探索，深受学生、督导和同行好评。

第二篇

1 课程优质教学设计

一、课程价值

（一）课程性质与目的

《英语学习策略与思维训练》作为英语专业基础阶段（一年级）专业核心能力必修课之一，旨在为学生提供英语学习和思维训练的方法指导，将思维技能和思维过程中所要用到的思维工具与英语语言知识学习和语言技能发展策略相结合，帮助学生在掌握理论知识的基础上，能够结合自己的学习进行实践，自觉将工具、策略和技能应用于学习过程，逐步养成良好的学习习惯和思维习惯。

（二）课程理念与思路

为最大化课程的人才培养价值，《英语学习策略与思维训练》以学习策略和思维训练的方法指导为使命，与同期开设的语言类课程共同构成 1+X 课程群，促进学习策略与思维训练双融入，从显性理解与初步运用到半显性二次理解与反复运用；采用"课前新知导学——课中体验应用——课后反思提升"的翻转教学模式，拓展课程学习和实训空间，辅助思维训练从低阶到高阶的有序融入和有效落地；依托蓝墨云班课移动教学助手，提供学习支持和记录学习过程；借助第三方学习平台，丰富学习资源和开展学习检测；增设课后专题指导与实践，促进学习困惑问题化，激发学习实践与研究意识。

（三）课程内容与任务

《英语学习策略与思维训练》课程共五章，从英语学习过程与支持系统入手，到英语语言知识学习策略与思维技能训练理论和实践，再到英语语言技能发展策略与思维技能训练理论与实践，理论与实践相结合，共计 30 学时，理论学时与实践学时各占 50%，详见表 1。

表 1 《英语学习策略与思维训练》课程章节构成与学时分配

章　　节	总学时	理论学时	实训学时
第一章　英语学习过程与支持系统	4	3	1
第二章　英语语言知识学习策略与思维技能训练理论	4	4	0
第三章　英语语言知识学习策略与思维技能训练实践	8	2	6
第四章　英语语言技能学习策略与思维技能训练理论	4	4	0
第五章　英语语言技能学习策略与思维技能训练实践	10	2	8
合　　计	30	15	15

《英语学习策略与思维训练》共五个章节，学习内容从人的学习行为模型、三大系统运作原理和学习策略与思维技能的定义和分类出发，逐步深入到英语语言知识学习和技能发展的理论基础：记忆模型运作原理、编码及其主要方式、图式、组块和思维可视化基本知识、语言知识学习和语言技能发展策略、技能与流程，再到英语语言知识学习和技能发

展的体验应用:学习流程体验与反思。全程强调"图式激活——理论输入——实践应用——反思提升",各章节学习任务主要围绕图式更新、实训打卡、反思总结等进行,具体包括每个章节的反思总结、理论章节的知识测试和案例分析评价、实训章节的计划制定、专项实训、期中反思报告、期末考核等,详见表2。

表 2 《英语学习策略与思维训练》课程章节内容与重难点

章　节	内　容	任　务
第一章 英语学习过程与支持系统	人的学习行为模型 自我系统、元认知系统、认知系统等的运作原理 学习策略与思维技能的定义与分类 结合英语学习情境,制订科学可行的英语学习计划	章节反思总结 理论知识测试 案例分析评价 学习计划制订
第二章 英语语言知识学习策略与思维技能训练理论	记忆模型运作原理 编码及其主要方式	章节反思总结 案例分析评价 理论知识测试 期中反思报告
第三章 英语语言知识学习策略与思维技能训练实践	词汇、语音、语法等语言知识学习策略 词汇、语音、语法等语言知识学习流程 语言知识学习思维过程、思维技能和思维工具	章节反思总结 词汇专项实训 语音专项实训 语法专项实训
第四章 英语语言技能发展策略与思维技能训练理论	图式运作原理 组块策略 思维可视化工具	章节反思总结 案例分析评价 理论知识测试
第五章 英语语言技能发展策略与思维技能训练实践	听力、阅读、写作、口语等语言技能发展策略 听力、阅读、写作、口语等语言技能发展流程 语言技能发展思维过程、思维技能和思维工具	章节反思总结 听力专项实训 阅读专项实训 写作专项实训 口语专项实训 期末考核

二、教学案例

(一)设计理念

《英语学习策略与思维训练》作为 1+X+Y 特色课程群的 1 课程,以显性化学习策略和思维训练方法指导为使命,旨在通过帮助学生提高学科素养、反思能力和沟通合作能力实现课程价值,具体包括:

学科素养方面:学生能了解人的学习行为模型、记忆模型、编码、图式、组块、思维可视化等基本理论,能掌握英语语言知识学习策略与思维技能和英语语言技能发展策略与思维技能,为同期开设的基础语言类课程和后续开设的职业类、文化类和学术类课程学习提供策略与方法。

反思能力方面：学生能在体验和实践英语语言知识学习策略与思维技能和英语语言技能发展策略与思维技能的过程中，结合人的学习行为模型、记忆模型、编码、图式、组块、思维可视化等基本理论知识，评价和反思自己的学习策略与方法，改进和养成良好的学习习惯和思维习惯。

沟通合作方面：学生能在理论学习、实践体验和反思提升的过程中，分享自己的学习经历与经验，表达自己的学习困难与需求，反馈自己的学习收获与思考，与他人共同发现英语语言知识学习和语言技能发展过程中存在的问题，共同实践和找到可行的策略和方法，形成良好的合作学习意识，建立可持续发展的学习共同体。

《英语学习策略与思维训练》课程理论略显枯燥且实践要求高，各章节学习采用"课前自主学习、课中体验应用、课后反思提升"方式实现翻转教学，提升课程教学效益。课前通过线上视频教学实现新知导学，帮助学生了解人的学习行为模型、记忆模型、编码、图式、组块、思维可视化等基本概念与内涵；课中通过对自主学习内容进行检测、答疑和补充进而开展学习流程体验，帮助学生体验学习计划制订、语言知识学习和语言技能发展过程；课后在课前和课中的基础上，通过结合自身学习经历进行反思总结，并完成理论知识检测、专项实训提升等，学生能够分享自己的学习经历与经验，表达自己的学习困难与需求，反馈自己的学习收获与思考，在安全的氛围中积极参与学习，大胆地思考、交流和分享，积极与同伴协作完成课程学习任务。

（二）代表课例

Development of English Learning Strategies and Thinking Skills
Unit 1 English Learning Process and Support Systems

Targets: Freshmen majoring in English education

Preparatory course: High School English

Parallel courses: Comprehensive English, English Viewing, Listening and Speaking

Prior learning: /

Materials: Self-compiled materials

Teaching Philosophy: Think-oriented & flipped learning

Durations: 4 periods

Objectives:

By the end of the session, students will be able

to **know about** the learning action model;

to **understand** the function mechanism of the self-system, the meta-cognition system and the cognition system;

to **know about** the definition and classification of learning strategies and thinking skills;

to **design** learning plans based on the self-learning situation.

Important/Difficult Point(s):

Understanding of the function mechanism of three systems;

Procedures of learning plan design.

Materials and Resources:

Handouts

Videoed lessons

Courseware

Computer and projector

Procedure:

Periods 1 & 2

Pre-class:

Step 1　Introduction to the course

Students watch the videoed lesson, **know about** the course, objectives, contents, tasks, assessments and participation requirements included, **raise questions and provide suggestions.**

Not clear about…

Hope… can be adapted in this / that way…

意图：通过课程导学微课，帮助建立课程认知，最小化认知障碍；通过提问和建议，创建师生平等学习氛围，激发学生学习兴趣，帮助学生打开自我系统。

Step 2　What would I do if I were Sam

Sam is going to memorize vocabulary for the participation of an important English test. What should he do? Students based on their own learning experience, standing in Sam's shoes, provide **suggestions** for him.

意图：通过建立情景任务，激发学生已有的相关图式，为学生在学习人的学习行为模型后对自己的学习行为进行评价提供依据。

Step 3   Introduction to the learning action model

- Students watch the videoed lesson, and **know about** the learning action model (Marzano, 2007):

  What is the learning action model about?

  What is the self-system?

  What is the meta-cognition system?

  What is the cognition system?

  How do the three systems function?

  How does knowledge help?

  Sample Analysis.

- Students **apply** the above and prepare for class **sharing:**

  Analysis of personal self-system functions;

  How does the personal meta-cognition system work in the process of a recent English learning program?

  In the process of completing a given multiple-choice, how does the personal cognition system work and what knowledge is adopted to help?

- Students **check** their personal understanding of the above and prepare for class **sharing:**

  How to test whether the self-system is open or not?

  Is the self-system important? And why or why not?

  Complete the sentence "The meta-cognition system is like…" and explain the reasons why you completed it like this.

意图：学生通过课前微课导学，了解人的学习行为模型、三大系统及其运作原理，并通过"学以致用"和"理解自查"任务尝试应用所学理论知识，检测对所学理论知识的理解，为课堂分享与讨论做好准备，为最大化课堂教学效益提供了保障；导学微课三步骤——"新知导学""学以致用"和"理解自查"形成了"学—用—评"闭环，为学生开展自主学习提供了示范，为养成良好的学习习惯和思维习惯打下基础。

While-class:

Step 1   About the course

Students **share** what they have **known / doubted** about the course, and what they would like to **suggest.**

The teacher facilitates to explain, organizes negotiation and fixes the teaching and learning calendar.

意图：通过师生协商，从源头上建立课程共同学习体，形成以学习为中心、以学生为主体的课程文化，再次助力学生自我系统的打开。

Step 2　Understanding and application: the learning action model

- Students **share** how they **apply and understand** the learning action model and the functioning of the three systems. The teacher facilitates to organize discussions, explains, and supplements relevant information.
- Students **analyze** and **evaluate** the given sample of how Michael learns based on the learning action model. The teacher makes comments accordingly.

意图：通过学生微课任务分享和案例分析评价以及教师答疑补充点评，帮助学生共同检测和发现理论知识理解上存在的问题，构建对理论知识和概念的正确理解，并形成良好的合作学习意识。

Step 3　Introduction to strategies and skills

- The teacher introduces the definition and categories of strategies and skills.
- Students **share** how they **apply and understand** strategies and skills in English learning. The teacher facilitates to organize discussions, explains, and supplements relevant information.

意图：通过课堂讲授、学生分享以及教师答疑补充点评，帮助学生学习新知识，构建对概念的正确理解，并形成良好的合作学习意识。

Post-class:

Step 1　Summary and feedback

Students **summarize** what they have learned, thought, and argued for/against in the two periods and provide their **feedback**. Peers read and **comment** on the given feedback.
—Learning action model
—Personal learning behavior

意图：学生通过总结、反馈和互评所学所思所疑，调动元认知系统运作，应用元认知学习策略，最大化课程学习共同体价值。

Step 2　What would I do if I were Sam

Sam is going to design a learning plan for the new semester. What should he do?
If you were Sam, what would you do?
Students based on their own learning experiences, provide **suggestions** for Sam.

意图：通过建立情景任务，激发学生已有的相关图式，为学生在规划小节学习后对自己制订的学习计划进行评价提供依据。

Step 3　Introduction to learning plan design

- Students watch the videoed lesson, and **know about** the suggested learning plan design procedure and supporting tools:

  Listing and choosing learning tasks;

  Setting and checking learning goals;

  Separating and arranging learning contents;

  Monitoring and recording learning processes;

  Analyzing and reflecting learning effects.

- Students **apply** the above and prepare for class **sharing**: What tools might be helpful in the process of learning plan design?

- Students **check** their personal understanding of the above and prepare for class **sharing**:

  In the procedure of learning plan design, which step(s) do you personally need to improve? Why? And how do you plan to improve?

意图：学生通过课前微课导学，了解学习计划制订流程与辅助工具；通过"学以致用"和"理解自查"任务，尝试应用所学理论知识，检测对所学理论知识的理解，为课堂分享与讨论做好准备；与此同时，"理解自查"环节为实训任务"学习计划制订"奠定了前期基础，找到了存在的问题，明确了改进的方向和内容。

Periods 3 & 4

While-class:

Step 1　Understanding and application: learning plan design

- Students **share** how they **apply** and **understand** the procedure for learning plan design. The teacher facilitates to organize discussion, explains, and supplements relevant information.

- Students **analyze** and **evaluate** the given sample of how Michael designs and carries out his learning plan. The teacher makes comments accordingly.

意图：通过学生微课任务分享和案例分析评价以及教师答疑补充点评，帮助学生共同检测和发现理论知识理解上存在的问题，构建对理论知识和概念的正确理解，并形成良好的合作学习意识。

Step 2　Experience and application: learning plan design

Students follow the procedure of learning plan design, experience and **practice** the design of learning plans step by step, focusing on the first three steps:

　　Listing and choosing learning tasks;

　　Setting and checking learning goals;

　　Separating and arranging learning contents.

意图：通过课堂体验应用，学生实训学习计划制订流程，重点实践自我系统分析、思维工具使用等，为课后尝试执行学习计划做准备。

Step 3　Questioning and quiz: Learning action model and learning plan design

- Students **raise questions** about what they doubt about the learning action model and learning plan design. The teacher facilitates to organize discussions, explains, and supplements relvant information.
- Students take part in the quiz about the learning action model and learning plan design. The teacher makes comments accordingly.

意图：通过学生提问、理论测试以及教师答疑讲评，帮助学生共同检测和发现理论知识理解上存在的问题，内化对理论知识和概念的正确理解，并形成良好的合作学习意识。

Post-class:

Step 1　Summary and feedback: learning plan design

Students **summarize** what they have learned, thought, and argued for/against in the two periods and provide their **feedback**. Peers read and **comment** on the given feedback.

—Learning plan design

—Personal experience

意图：学生通过总结、反馈和互评所学所思所疑，强化元认知意识，逐步提升元认知水平。

Step 2　Further practice: Learning Plan

Students follow the designed learning plan, **practice** the last two steps, and hand in the practice report.

—Monitoring and recording learning processes;

—Analyzing and reflecting learning effects.

意图：通过执行学习计划，尝试监控、记录、分析和反思，在实践中建立对学习计划制订的正确认知，迈出养成良好学习习惯的关键一步。

Unit 2   Theories for English Language Knowledge Development: Learning Strategies and Thinking Skills

Targets: Freshmen majoring in English education

Preparatory course: High School English

Parallel courses: Comprehensive English, English Viewing, Listening and Speaking

Prior learning: Learning Action Model

Materials: Self-compiled materials

Teaching Philosophy: Think-oriented & flipped learning

Durations: 4 periods

Objectives:

By the end of the session, students will be able

to **know about** the memory model;

to **familiarize** the definition and main forms of encoding;

Important/Difficult Point(s):

Understanding the connections and differences between short-term memory, long-term memory and working memory;

Understanding the connections and differences between stimuli, attention, encoding, rehearse and retrieve;

Application of encoding.

Materials and Resources:

Handouts

Videoed lessons

Courseware

Computer and projector

Procedure:

<u>Periods 1 & 2</u>

Pre-class:

Step 1　Introduction to the memory model

- Students watch the videoed lesson, and **know about** the memory model of the Atkinson-Shiffrin Model:

  How does memory work?

  What is sensory memory?

  What is short-term memory?

  What is long-term memory?

  What is working-memory?

  What are the key elements in the memory process?

意图：学生通过课前微课导学，了解记忆模型；通过"学以致用"和"理解自查"任务尝试应用所学理论知识，检测对所学理论知识的理解，为课堂分享与讨论做好准备。

Step 2　Sample analysis

- Students **apply** the above and prepare for class **sharing**:

  Interpret the given picture using the memory model.

- Students **check** their personal understanding of the above and prepare for class **sharing**:

  What is the name of the learned memory model?

  What is the relationship among sensory memory, short-term memory, working memory and long-term memory?

  Clarify your understanding of the memory model using your personal experience or story.

While-class:

Step 1　Understanding and application: the memory model

- Students **share** how they understand the memory model and the functioning of the four types of memory. The teacher facilitates to organize discussions, explains, and supplements relevant information.

- Students **analyze** and **interpret** the given picture based on the memory model. The teacher makes comments accordingly.

意图：通过学生微课任务分享和教师答疑补充点评，帮助学生共同检测和发现理论知识理解上存在的问题，构建对理论知识和概念的正确理解，并形成良好的合作学习意识。

Step 2　How does Sam's memory system work

Students **analyze** and **share** how Sam's memory system works based on the given sample of his English learning.

意图：通过 Sam 的英语学习过程案例分析，帮助学生加深对记忆系统工作原理的理解。

Step 3　Questioning and quiz: the memory model

● Students **raise questions** about what they doubt about the memory model. The teacher facilitates to organize discussions, explains, and supplements relevant information.

● Students take part in the quiz about the memory model. The teacher makes comments accordingly.

意图：通过学生提问、理论测试以及教师答疑讲评，帮助学生共同检测和发现理论知识理解上存在的问题，内化对理论知识和概念的正确理解，并形成良好的合作学习意识。

Post-class:

Step 1　Summary and feedback

Students **summarize** what they have learned, thought, and argued for/against in the two periods and provide their **feedback**. Peers read and **comment** on the given feedback.
—Memory model

意图：学生通过总结、反馈和互评所学所思所疑，调动元认知系统运作，应用元认知学习策略，最大化课程学习共同体价值。

Step 2　Introduction to encoding

● Students watch the videoed lesson, and **know about** the five encoding methods:

What is encoding?

How does encoding function in memory?

Semantic encoding;

Visual encoding;

Acoustic encoding;

Encoding through other senses;

Elaborative encoding.

意图：学生通过课前微课导学，了解编码的定义、功能和主要方式；通过"学以致用"和"理解自查"任务尝试应用所学理论知识，检测对所学理论知识的理解，为课堂分享与讨论做好准备。

- Students **apply** the above and prepare for class **sharing:**
  How to encode the given three words and thus better memorize them?
- Students **check** personal understanding of the above and prepare for class **sharing**:
  How do the following four words connect and associate in your understanding: acoustic, semantic, visual and elaborative?
  Draw a picture to show your understanding of encoding;
  List 3 encoding examples in your English learning process.

Periods 3 & 4

While-class:

Step 1   Understanding and application: encoding

- Students **share** how they **apply** and **understand** the definition, function and main methods of encoding. The teacher facilitates to organize discussion, explain, and supplement.
- Students **analyze** and **share** how to encode the given four words. The teacher makes comments accordingly.

意图：通过学生微课任务分享和教师答疑补充点评，帮助学生共同检测和发现理论知识理解上存在的问题，构建对理论知识和概念的正确理解，并形成良好的合作学习意识。

Step 2   Experience and application: encoding

Students experience and practice the mixed use of encoding methods for different sample words:

意图：通过课堂体验编码方式的混合应用，学生实训混合式编码，帮助进一步熟悉主要的编码方式。

Step 3　Questioning and quiz: encoding

- Students **raise questions** about what they doubt about encoding. The teacher facilitates to organize discussions, explains, and supplements relevant information.
- Students take part in the quiz about encoding. The teacher makes comments accordingly.

意图：通过学生提问、理论测试以及教师答疑讲评，帮助学生共同检测和发现理论知识理解上存在的问题，内化对理论知识和概念的正确理解，并形成良好的合作学习意识。

Post-class:

Step 1　Summary and feedback

Students **summarize** what they have learned, thought, and argued for/against in the two periods and provide their **feedback**. Peers read and **comment** on the given feedback.

—Encoding

—Mixed use of encoding methods

意图：学生通过总结、反馈和互评所学所思所疑，强化元认知意识，逐步提升元认知水平。

Step 2　Further practice: encoding

Students try to **encode** more words and be familiar with the mixed use of encoding methods.

意图：通过课后编码训练，尝试改进词汇学习，养成"学以致用"的良好学习习惯，为下一章节的词汇学习奠定基础。

Unit 3　Practice for English Language Knowledge Development: Learning Strategies and Thinking Skills

Targets: Freshmen majoring in English education

Preparatory course: High School English

Parallel courses: Comprehensive English, English Viewing, Listening and Speaking

Prior learning: Learning action model, Memory model and Encoding

Materials: Self-compiled materials

Teaching Philosophy: Think-oriented & flipped learning

Durations: 6 periods

Objectives:

By the end of the session, students will be able

to **recall and reflect** their previous language knowledge learning experience;

to put theories from prior learning into practice;

to **experience and practice** the process for effective vocabulary, pronunciation and grammar learning

Important/Difficult Point(s):

Application of related theories;

Practice of new language knowledge learning strategies.

Materials and Resources:

Handouts

Videoed lessons

Courseware

Computer and projector

Procedure:

<u>Periods 1 & 2</u>

Pre-class:

Step 1   What would I do if I were Sam

Sam is going to memorize vocabulary for the participation of an important English test. What should he do? Students based on their own learning experience, standing in Sam's shoes, provide **suggestions** for him.

意图：通过建立情景任务，让学生回忆自己的单词记忆经验，便于与后续所学的单词学习策略进行对比。

Step 2   Introduction to the vocabulary learning process

- Students watch the videoed lesson, and **know about** the vocabulary learning process:

  Plan & judge;

  Classify & encode;

  Retrieve & rehearse;

  Apply & consolidate.

- Students **apply** the above and prepare for class sharing:

  Pick up 20 words from your English textbook randomly and judge: what are active vocabularies, what are passive vocabularies and what are super passive vocabularies?

  How is encoding used in the given examples?

  What methods will you use to retrieve the given words?

- Students **check** their personal understanding of the above and prepare for class **sharing**:

  What's the link between plan and judge?

  How do plan and judge help with the efficiency of vocabulary learning?

  How does encoding help in promoting vocabulary memory?

  What are the similarities and differences between retrieve & rehears and apply & consolidate?

意图：学生通过课前微课导学，了解单词学习步骤，即"计划与判断—分类与编码—复述与提取—应用与巩固"；通过"学以致用"和"理解自查"任务尝试应用所学知识，检测对所学知识的理解，为课堂分享与讨论做好准备。

While-class:

Step 1 Understanding and application: vocabulary learning strategies

Students **share** how they **apply and understand** the process of vocabulary learning and corresponding strategies. The teacher facilitates to organize discussions, explains, and supplements relevant information.

意图：通过学生微课任务分享及教师答疑补充点评，帮助学生发现语言知识学习策略上存在的问题，构建正确理解，并形成良好的合作学习意识。

Step 2 Experience and application: vocabulary learning strategies

Students follow the procedure of vocabulary learning, experience and **practice** it step by step:

● The 1st round of vocabulary learning (with handouts):

(1) Students will be given 5 minutes to try in their usual way to deal with words and expressions given on handouts (from Unit 2 Comprehensive English 1) and have a quiz to check their learning afterwards;

(2) Students will be asked to share their process of vocabulary learning to see if any strategies/methods have been used.

● The 2nd round of vocabulary learning: Students are going to remember given words and expressions again by following the 4-step process and finish a quiz again.

● Compare the vocabulary learning process in Round 1 and that in Round 2.

意图：通过课堂体验应用，学生实训单词学习的过程，并通过针对同一组单词的两轮测试，对比传统学习方法和融合了思维训练的、有步骤的单词学习新策略，进一步体验后者如何有效地改善学习效果。

Post-class:

Step 1 Summary and feedback

Students **summarize** what they have learned, thought, and argued for/against in the two periods and provide their **feedback**. Peers read and **comment** on the given feedback.

—Vocabulary learning process

意图：学生通过总结、反馈和互评所学所思所疑，回顾单词学习过程，最大化掌握单词学习策略。

Step 2　Further practice

Students **design** their own vocabulary learning plan and refer to the textbook from other courses. They should follow their designed plan and **practice** the vocabulary learning process.

意图：学生在课后自行选择相关专业课，如综合英语、英语视听说、英语阅读等课程，制定单词学习计划，进一步巩固和练习单词学习的步骤和策略，完成实训打卡任务。

Periods 3 & 4

Pre-class:

Step 1　Self-analysis

Students recall their pronunciation learning experiences and list their difficulties. They can use different thinking maps to organize their thinking.

意图：让学生回忆语音学习过程中的困难，并整理困难，以便后续在语音学习过程中进行解决。

Step 2　Introduction to the pronunciation learning process (phonemes)

- Students watch the videoed lesson, and **know about** the pronunciation learning process (phonemes):
  Entry test
  Spotting the difficult phonemes
  Encoding for discrimination
  Rehearsing
  Exit test
- Students **apply** the above and prepare for class sharing:
  Find out your difficult phonemes.
  What encoding methods you can use to distinguish between /v/ and /f/?
  How do you rehearse the difficult phonemes you spot above?
- Students **check** their personal understanding of the above and prepare for class **sharing**:
  What are effective encoding approaches in the pronunciation learning process of phonemes?

意图：学生通过课前微课导学，了解语音音素学习步骤，即"前测—困难音素定位—辨音编码—复述—后测"；通过"学以致用"和"理解自查"任务尝试应用所学知识，检测对所学知识的理解，为课堂分享与讨论做好准备。

Step 3 Introduction to the pronunciation learning process (rules)

- Students watch the videoed lesson, and **know about** the pronunciation learning process (rules):

  Entry test

  Listing difficulties

  Organizing difficulties

  Seeking rules

  Interpreting and visualizing rules

  Exemplifying

  Exit test

- Students **apply** the above and prepare for class sharing:

  What difficulties do you have in studying the pronunciation rule of linking?

  What methods can you use to visualize the rules you find and make it easier to understand and remember?

- Students **check** their personal understanding of the above and prepare for class **sharing**:

  What are the similarities and differences between the vocabulary learning process and the pronunciation learning process?

意图：学生通过课前微课导学，了解语音规则学习步骤，即"前测—困难清单—困难梳理—规则查找—规则理解—举例说明—后测"；通过"学以致用"和"理解自查"任务尝试应用所学知识，检测对所学知识的理解，为课堂分享与讨论做好准备。

While-class:

Step 1 Understanding and application: pronunciation learning strategies

Students **share** how they **apply and understand** the process of pronunciation learning and corresponding strategies. The teacher facilitates to organize discussion, explains, and supplements relevant information.

意图：通过学生微课任务分享及教师答疑补充点评，帮助学生发现语言知识学习策略上存在的问题，构建正确理解，并形成良好的合作学习意识。

Step 2 Experience and application: pronunciation learning strategies

Students follow the procedure of pronunciation learning, experience and **practice** it step by step:

- The pronunciation learning process (phonemes)
  Entry test: spotting difficult phonemes
  Practice: minimal-pair
  Encoding
  Rehearse
  Exit test: checking learning effect
- The pronunciation learning process (rules)
  Entry test: spotting difficult linking.
  Taking linking as an example, students work in groups and explore how to employ learning strategies and thinking skills into the pronunciation learning process, on the basis of their knowledge of the learning action model, the memory system and encoding.
  Exit test: checking learning effects.

意图：通过课堂体验应用，学生实训语音学习的过程。语音音素部分通过教师提供的前测素材定位困难音素、以 minimal-pair 相关素材进行辨音和编码练习，以后测素材检验学习效果；语音规则部分以连读为例，提供讲解材料让学生定位困难、整理规则、用思考图呈现规则等。实训环节可以让学生充分体验完整的语音学习过程。

Post-class:

Step 1 Summary and feedback

Students **summarize** what they have learned, thought, and argued for/against in the two periods and provide their **feedback**. Peers read and **comment** on the given feedback.
—Pronunciation learning process

意图：学生通过总结、反馈和互评所学所思所疑，回顾语音学习过程，最大化掌握语音学习策略。

Step 2 Further practice

Students **design** their own pronunciation learning plans and refer to the textbook from their English Pronunciation Lesson. They should follow their designed plan and **practice** the pronunciation learning process.

意图：学生在课后参考语音课教材和课堂学习内容，制订语音学习计划，进一步巩固和练习语音音素和语音规则的学习策略，完成实训打卡任务。

Periods 5 & 6

Pre-class:

Step 1　Self-analysis

Students recall their grammar learning experiences and list their difficulties. They can use different thinking maps to organize their thinking.

意图：让学生回忆语法学习过程中的困难，并整理困难，以便后续在语音学习过程中进行解决。

Step 2　Introduction to the grammar learning process

- Students watch the videoed lesson, and **know about** grammar learning process:

  Entry test

  Seeking rules

  Interpreting and visualizing rules

  Exemplifying

  Exit test

- Students **apply** the above and prepare for class sharing:

  What is noun clause, and what are the grammar rules you can find about noun clause?

  How do you organize the grammar rules of noun clause?

- Students **check** their personal understanding of the above and prepare for class **sharing**:

  What's the role of encoding in the grammar learning process?

  What thinking tools can you use in the grammar learning process?

  What are the similarities and differences between the process of learning grammar rules and the process of learning phonetic rules?

意图：学生通过课前微课导学，了解语法学习步骤，即"前测—规则查找—规则理解—举例说明—后测"；通过"学以致用"和"理解自查"任务尝试应用所学理论知识，检测对所学理论知识的理解，为课堂分享与讨论做好准备。

While-class:

Step 1 Understanding and application: grammar learning strategies

Students **share** how they **apply and understand** the process of grammar learning and corresponding strategies. The teacher facilitates to organize discussion, explains, and supplements relevant information.

意图：通过学生微课任务分享及教师答疑补充点评，帮助学生发现语言知识学习策略上存在的问题，构建正确理解，并形成良好的合作学习意识。

Step 2 Experience and application: grammar learning strategies

Students follow the procedure of grammar learning, experience and **practice** it step by step:

- Entry test: finish a quiz of noun (20 multiple choices) and spot difficult grammar rules.
- Taking the comparison between uncountable nouns and countable nouns as an example, students work in groups to seek rules by referring to a chosen grammar book and explore how to employ learning strategies and thinking skills into the grammar learning process. During the task, the double bubble map is introduced and adapted as a thinking tool.
- Exit test: checking learning effects.

意图：通过课堂体验应用，学生实训语法学习的过程，以名词规则为例，进行规则查找，并使用双气泡图整理可数名词与不可数名词的区别。学生也可以尝试使用其他思维工具整理语法规则，强化语法学习效果。

Post-class:

Step 1 Summary and feedback

Students **summarize** what they have learned, thought, and argued for/against in the two periods and provide their **feedback**. Peers read and **comment** on the given feedback.
—Grammar learning process

意图：学生通过总结、反馈和互评所学所思所疑，回顾语法学习过程，最大化掌握单词学习策略。

Step 2　Further practice

Students **design** their own grammar learning plans and refer to the textbook from their Grammar Lesson. They should follow their designed plans and **practice** the grammar learning process.

意图：学生在课后参考语法课教材和课堂学习内容，制定语法学习计划，进一步巩固语法学习策略，查漏补缺，完成实训打卡任务。

Unit 4　Theories for English Language Skills Development: Learning Strategies and Thinking Skills

Targets: Freshmen majoring in English education

Preparatory course: High School English

Parallel courses: Comprehensive English, English Viewing, Listening and Speaking

Prior learning: /

Materials: Self-compiled materials

Teaching Philosophy: Think-oriented & flipped learning

Durations: 4 periods

Objectives:

By the end of the session, students will be able

to **know about** the definition and application of schema;

to **know about** the definition and application of chunking;

to **know about** the definition and application of thinking visualization and representative tools.

Important/Difficult Point(s):

Application of schema and chunking;

Proper selection of thinking visualization tools.

Materials and Resources:

Handouts

Videoed lessons

Courseware

Computer and projector

Procedure:

<u>**Periods 1 & 2**</u>

Pre-class:

Step 1   Introduction to schema

- Students watch the videoed lesson, and **know about** schema:

  What is schema?

  How does schema function in English learning?

  What are key elements in the memory process?

  Sample Analysis

- Students **apply** the above and prepare for class **sharing**:

  Interpret the given picture using personal knowledge and experiences.

- Students **check** their personal understanding of the above and prepare for class **sharing**:

  What is schema?

  How schema is used in personal English learning?

  Give examples.

意图：学生通过课前微课导学，了解图式的定义及其在外语教学中的应用；通过"学以致用"和"理解自查"任务尝试应用所学理论知识，检测对所学理论知识的理解，为课堂分享与讨论做好准备。

Step 2   Introduction to chunking

- Students watch the videoed lesson, and **know about** chunking:

  What is chunking?

  Significance for chunking;

  Strategies for chunking.

- Students **apply** the above and prepare for class **sharing**:

  Analyze the given paragraphs using proper chunking strategies;

  Prepare a paragraph of about 50 words and practice how to use proper chunking strategies for better memory.

- Students **check** their personal understanding of the above and prepare for class **sharing**:

  What does "7" mean in chunking?

  What strategies can be used for chunking?

  Give examples.

意图：学生通过课前微课导学，了解组块的定义及其在外语教学中的应用策略；通过"学以致用"和"理解自查"任务尝试应用所学理论知识，检测对所学理论知识的理解，为课堂分享与讨论做好准备。

While-class:

Step 1   Understanding and application: schema

- Students **share** how they understand schema and the application of schema in English learning. The teacher facilitates to organize discussion, explains, and supplements relevant information.
- Students **analyze** and **interpret** the given picture based on the schema theory. The teacher makes comments accordingly.

意图：通过学生微课任务分享和教师答疑补充点评，帮助学生共同检测和发现理论知识理解上存在的问题，构建对理论知识和概念的正确理解，并形成良好的合作学习意识。

Step 2   Understanding and application: chunking

- Students **share** how they understand chunking and the application of schema in English learning. The teacher facilitates to organize discussion, explains, and supplements relevant information.
- Students **analyze** and **interpret** the given paragraphs based on the chunking strategies. The teacher makes comments accordingly.

意图：通过学生微课任务分享和教师答疑补充点评，帮助学生共同检测和发现理论知识理解上存在的问题，构建对理论知识和概念的正确理解，并形成良好的合作学习意识。

Step 3   Questioning and quiz: schema and chunking

- Students **raise questions** about what they doubt about schema and chunking. The teacher facilitates to organize discussions, explains, and supplements relevant information.
- Students take part in the quiz about schema and chunking. The teacher makes comments accordingly.

意图：通过学生提问、理论测试以及教师答疑讲评，帮助学生共同检测和发现理论知识理解上存在的问题，内化对理论知识和概念的正确理解，并形成良好的合作学习意识。

Post-class:

Step 1   Summary and feedback

Students **summarize** what they have learned, thought, and argued for/against in the two periods and provide their **feedback**. Peers read and **comment** on the given feedback.
—Schema
—Chunking

意图：学生通过总结、反馈和互评所学所思所疑，调动元认知系统运作，应用元认知学习策略，最大化课程学习共同体价值。

Step 2   Introduction to thinking visualization tools:

mind-map, concept-map and thinking-map

- Students watch the videoed lesson, and **know about** thinking visualization and representative tools:

  What is thinking visualization?

  Mind-map;

  Concept-map;

  Thinking-map.

- Students **apply** the above and prepare for class **sharing**:

  How to take notes using a mind-map?

  Match the proper visualization tool to the learning context.

  What skill does each map help to present?

- Students **check** their personal understanding of the above and prepare for class **sharing**:

  What should be taken into consideration when making different maps?

  What are the differences and similarities between mind-map and concept-map?

  Which map are you familiar with the most?

  Give an example of how you use it in English learning.

意图：学生通过课前微课导学，了解思维可视化及其代表性工具——思维导图、概念图和八大思维图示；通过"学以致用"和"理解自查"任务尝试应用所学理论知识，检测对所学理论知识的理解，为课堂分享与讨论做好准备。

Periods 3 & 4

While-class:

Step 1   Understanding and application: thinking visualization tools

- Students **share** how they **apply** and **understand** the three representative thinking visualization tools. The teacher facilitates to organize discussions, explains, and supplements relevant information.

- Students **analyze** and **share** how they use proper thinking visualization tools for different learning contexts. The teacher makes comments accordingly.

意图：通过学生微课任务分享和教师答疑补充点评，帮助学生共同检测和发现理论知识理解上存在的问题，构建对理论知识和概念的正确理解，并形成良好的合作学习意识。

Step 2　Experience and application: thinking visualization tools

Students experience and practice the mixed use of thinking visualization tools for different learning contexts.

意图：通过课堂体验思维可视化工具的混合应用，学生实训复杂思维过程图示，进一步熟悉主要的思维可视化工具的灵活应用。

Step 3　Questioning and quiz: thinking visualization tools

- Students **raise questions** about what they doubt about thinking visualization tools. The teacher facilitates to organize discussion, explains, and supplements relevant information.
- Students take part in the quiz about thinking visualization tools. The teacher makes comments accordingly.

意图：通过学生提问、理论测试以及教师答疑讲评，帮助学生共同检测和发现理论知识理解上存在的问题，内化对理论知识和概念的正确理解，并形成良好的合作学习意识。

Post-class:

Step 1　Summary and feedback

Students **summarize** what they have learned, thought, and argued for/against in the two periods and provide their **feedback**. Peers read and **comment** on the given feedback.
—Mind-map
—Concept-map
—Thinking-map

意图：学生通过总结、反馈和互评所学所思所疑，强化元认知意识，逐步提升元认知水平。

Step 2　Further practice: thinking visualization tools

Students try to **use proper** visualization tools for more contexts in English learning and get ready for the following of language skills development.

意图：通过课后可视化工具应用训练，养成"学以致用"的良好学习习惯，为下一章节的语言技能发展奠定基础。

Unit 5 Practice for English Language Skills Development: Learning Strategies and Thinking Skills

Targets: Freshmen majoring in English education

Preparatory course: High School English

Parallel courses: Comprehensive English, English Viewing, Listening and Speaking

Prior learning: Learning action model, Memory model, Encoding, Schema, Chunking, Thinking visualization tools

Materials: Self-compiled materials

Teaching Philosophy: Think-oriented & flipped learning

Durations: 8 periods

Objectives:

By the end of the session, students will be able

to **recall and reflect** their previous language skills learning experiences;

to put theories from prior learning into practice;

to **experience and practice** the process for effective listening, reading, writing and speaking learning.

Important/Difficult Point(s):

Application of related theories;

Practice of new language skills learning strategies.

Materials and Resources:

Handouts

Videoed lessons

Courseware

Computer and projector

Procedure:

<u>Periods 1 & 2</u>

Pre-class:

Step 1　Self-analysis

- Students complete a questionnaire to figure out their listening learning style.
- Students recall their listening learning experiences and list their difficulties. They can use different thinking maps to organize their thinking.

意图：学生自行完成问卷调查，了解自己的听力学习风格，并回忆听力学习过程中的困难，继而整理困难，便于后续在听力学习过程中进行解决。

Step 2　Introduction to the listening learning process

- Students watch the videoed lesson, and **know about** the listening learning process:

Pre-listening: set listening objectives, activate schema, predict possible answers, analyze and compare different choices…

While-listening: monitor the listening process, verify predictions, adjust attention distribution, take down notes…

Post-listening: evaluate and reflect, edit and revise…

- Students **apply** the above and prepare for class sharing:

Read the choices of the following conversations, and predict the possible topics and language expressions.

What information do you collect when listening to the following conversations?

After listening to the following conversations, how do you reflect and evaluate on them?

- Students **check** their personal understanding of the above and prepare for class **sharing**:

What you can do to improve the efficiency of activating schema in the pre-listening stage?

How do you apply chunking in the while-listening stage?

Of the pre-listening, listening, and post-listening strategies and skills, which do you think helped you the most?

意图：学生通过课前微课导学，了解听力学习过程，即"听前—听中—听后"，以及每个阶段下面的具体策略；通过"学以致用"和"理解自查"任务尝试应用所学知识，检测对所学知识的理解，为课堂分享与讨论做好准备。

While-class:

Step 1   Understanding and application: listening learning strategies

Students **share** how they **apply and understand** the process of listening learning and corresponding strategies. The teacher facilitates to organize discussion, explains, and supplements relevant information.

意图：通过学生微课任务分享及教师答疑补充点评，帮助学生发现语言技能学习策略上存在的问题，构建正确理解，并形成良好的合作学习意识。

Step 2   Experience and application: listening learning strategies

Students follow the procedure of listening learning through different listening tasks, experience and **practice** the process step by step.

- Task 1:

  Watch the beginning part of *video That's why I chose Yale*;

  Use concept maps to recall ideas and knowledge with schema;

  Share your prediction in groups;

  Finish watching the video to verify your prediction.
- Task 2: Blank filling
- Task 3: Multiple choices

  News reports

  Conversations
- Self-reflection

  Students will use the checklist to reflect their listening process.

意图：通过课堂体验应用，学生实训听力学习的过程。实训过程中，学生需要完成不同类型的听力任务，在每个听力任务中完整体验"听前—听中—听后"三大步骤，并利用清单来检验每个步骤的完成情况，强化听力学习效果。

Checklist:	
<u>Pre-listening</u>	
□ set listening objectives	□ analyze and compare different choices
□ activate schema	□ summarize and infer
□ predict possible answers	□ arrange attention distribution
<u>While-listening</u>	
□ monitor listening process	□ be aware of cognitive operations
□ verify predictions	□ take down notes
□ adjust attention distribution	
<u>Post-listening</u>	
□ evaluate and reflect	
□ edit and revise	

Post-class:

Step 1   Summary and feedback

Students **summarize** what they have learned, thought, and argued for/against in the two periods and provide their **feedback**. Peers read and **comment** on the given feedback.
—Listening learning process

意图：学生通过总结、反馈和互评所学所思所疑，回顾听力学习过程，最大化掌握听力学习策略。

Step 2   Further practice

Students **design** their own listening learning plan and refer to the textbook from their Listening Lesson. They should follow their designed plan and **practice** the listening learning process.

意图：学生在课后参考英语视听说课教材和课堂学习内容，制定听力学习计划，进一步巩固听力学习策略，完成实训打卡任务。

Periods 3 & 4

Pre-class:

Step 1   Self-analysis

- Students complete a questionnaire to figure out their reading learning style.
- Students recall their reading learning experiences and list their difficulties. They can use different thinking maps to organize their thinking.

意图：学生自行完成问卷调查，了解自己的阅读学习风格，并回忆阅读学习过程中的困难，继而整理困难，便于后续在阅读学习过程中进行解决。

Step 2   Introduction to the reading learning process

- Students watch the videoed lesson, and **know about** the reading learning process:
  Pre-reading: activate schema, predict possible answers…
  While-reading: skimming, scanning, making an inference, process monitoring…
  Post-reading: evaluate and reflect, summarize and improve…
- Students **apply** the above and prepare for class sharing:
  From the first sentence of the given passage, what do you know about "college studies"?

意图：学生通过课前微课导学，了解阅读学习过程，即"读前—读中—读后"，以及每个阶段下面的具体策略；通过"学以致用"和"理解自查"任务尝试应用所学知识，检测对所学知识的理解，为课堂分享与讨论做好准备。

By reading the first sentence of the other paragraph, "There are three reasons why some students cannot finish their college studies", what might be the reasons in your opinion?

Complete the following reading practice, and record while-reading strategies used and the specific examples on your notebook.

What methods can you summarize after finishing the reading practice above?

- Students **check** their personal understanding of the above and prepare for class **sharing**:

How can you effectively activate your schema in the pre-reading stage?

How can you be flexible with skimming and scanning in your reading?

Which of the pre-reading, while-reading and post-reading strategies do you find most helpful?

While-class:

Step 1　Understanding and application: reading learning strategies

Students **share** how they **apply and understand** the process of reading learning and corresponding strategies. The teacher facilitates to organize discussions, explains, and supplements relevant information.

意图：通过学生微课任务分享及教师答疑补充点评，帮助学生发现语言技能学习策略上存在的问题，构建正确理解，并形成良好的合作学习意识。

Step 2 Experience and application: reading learning strategies

Students follow the procedure of reading learning through different reading tasks, experience and **practice** the process step by step:

The Message Behind the Smile
(from Unit 8 *Comprehensive English 1*)

- Pre-reading: activate schema & predict:

  What knowledge or experience can you think of about the given topic?

  What genre might it belong to?

  What might it talk about?

  How might the structure be?

- While-reading:

  Trace (name, place, time, topic sentence, signals, highlights…)

  Analyze (structure, paragraph idea, long and difficult sentences, figure of speech…)

  Infer

  Paraphrase

- Post-reading: Reflect from the following aspects:

  Reading process

  Reading types

  Reading support

- Group work: choose one of the following two texts:

  The Mystery of the White Gardenia (from Unit 7 *of Comprehensive English 1*)

  The Risk of Life (from Unit 10 *of Comprehensive English 1*)

  and

  Activate schema

  Predict genre, content and structure

  Finish the comprehension exercise

  Process reflection: strategy and skill

意图：通过课堂体验应用，学生实训阅读学习的过程，完整体验"读前—读中—读后"三大步骤。教师鼓励学生调用图式理论对文本进行推断预测，并根据文章体裁和结构，运用不同类型的思考图进行分析。教师为学生提供不同视角，引导学生对文本内容进行分析，并协助学生反思阅读过程。示范体验后，学生分小组自行选择篇目再次实践，在实践中熟悉相应的学习策略。

Post-class:

Step 1   Summary and feedback

Students **summarize** what they have learned, thought, and argued for/against in the two periods and provide their **feedback**. Peers read and **comment** on the given feedback. —Reading learning process

意图：学生通过总结、反馈和互评所学所思所疑，回顾阅读学习过程，最大化掌握阅读学习策略。

Step 2   Further practice

Students **design** their own reading learning plan and refer to the textbook from their Reading Lesson. They should follow their designed plan and **practice** the reading learning process.

意图：学生在课后参考英语阅读课教材和课堂学习内容，制定阅读学习计划，进一步巩固阅读学习策略，完成实训打卡任务。

Periods 5 & 6

Pre-class:

Step 1   Self-analysis

- Students complete a questionnaire to figure out their writing learning style.
- Students recall their writing learning experiences and list their difficulties. They can use different thinking maps to organize their thinking.

意图：学生自行完成问卷调查，了解自己的写作学习风格，并回忆在写作学习过程中的困难，继而整理困难，以便后续在写作学习过程中解决。

Step 2   Introduction to the writing learning process

- Students watch the videoed lesson, and **know about** the writing learning process:
  Pre-writing: idea preparation, goal setting, information collection, thought organization…
  While-writing: lexical diversity, lexical accuracy, syntactic diversity, cohesion & coherence, monitoring strategies…
  Post-writing: check & revise, reflect & improve…

意图：学生通过课前微课导学，了解写作学习过程，即"写前—写中—写后"，以及每个阶段下面的具体策略；通过"学以致用"和"理解自查"任务尝试应用所学知识，检测对所学知识的理解，为课堂分享与讨论做好准备。

- Students **apply** the above and prepare for class sharing:
  If you're going to write an essay about travel, what can you do in the pre-writing stage?
  For this part, you are allowed 15 minutes to write a paragraph about how to best handle the relationship between parents and children. Try to apply lexical diversity, lexical accuracy, syntactic diversity, cohesion & coherence and monitoring strategies when you write.
  Can you summarize the methods to elaborate an argument after finishing the writing practice above?
- Students **check** their personal understanding of the above and prepare for class **sharing**:
  How do you effectively organize your thoughts in the pre-writing stage?
  What part in the while-writing stage do you find most difficult? Is there any way to improve it?
  Which of the pre-writing, while-writing and post-writing strategies do you find most helpful?

While-class:

Step 1　Understanding and application: writing learning strategies

Students **share** how they **apply and understand** the process of writing learning and corresponding strategies. The teacher facilitates to organize discussion, explains, and supplements relevant information.

意图：通过学生微课任务分享及教师答疑补充点评，帮助学生发现语言技能学习策略上存在的问题，构建正确理解，并形成良好的合作学习意识。

Step 2   Experience and application: writing learning strategies

Students follow the procedure of writing learning, experience and **practice** the process step by step:

- Pre-writing

    Idea preparation: How much do you know about "name"?

    Goal setting: If to write about "name", what title would you like to work on? What genre does your proposed writing belong to?

    Information collection: What information beyond schema have you got for the proposed writing?

    Thoughts organization: What skills may help you to organize all the needed information? Which thinking map(s) might help visualize your thinking?

    Outline production: thesis statement and supporting details

- While-writing

    Write an essay around the topic "name" and follow the outline you make in the pre-writing stage. Pay attention to lexical diversity, lexical accuracy, syntactic diversity as well as cohesion and coherence in your writing.

- Post-writing

    Evaluating and checking: check list;

    Editing and revising;

    Recalling and reflecting

Post-class:

Step 1   Summary and feedback

Students **summarize** what they have learned, thought, and argued for/against in the two periods and provide their **feedback**. Peers read and **comment** on the given feedback.

—Writing learning process

意图：通过课堂体验应用，学生实训写作学习的过程，完整体验"写前—写中—写后"三大步骤。教师以学生综合英语课教材中相关单元话题"名字"为主题，启发学生从不同角度、不同文体思考可能写作的内容，鼓励学生运用不同类型的思考图构思写作大纲，并根据大纲完成写作，在实践中熟悉相应的学习策略。

意图：学生通过总结、反馈和互评所学所思所疑，回顾写作学习过程，最大化掌握写作学习策略。

Step 2　Further practice

Students **design** their own writing learning plan and refer to the textbook from their Writing Lesson. They should follow their designed plan and **practice** the writing learning process.

意图：学生在课后参考英语写作课教材和课堂学习内容，也可以结合阅读实训打卡的内容，将阅读与写作的话题结合起来，制定写作学习计划，进一步巩固写作学习策略，完成实训打卡任务。

Periods 7 & 8

Pre-class:

Step 1　Self-analysis

- Students complete a questionnaire to figure out their speaking learning style.
- Students recall their speaking learning experiences and list their difficulties. They can use different thinking maps to organize their thinking.

意图：学生自行完成问卷调查，了解自己的口语学习风格，并回忆口语学习过程中的困难，继而整理困难，以便后续在口语学习过程中进行解决。

Step 2　Introduction to the speaking learning process

- Students watch the videoed lesson, and **know about** the speaking learning process:

  Pre-speaking: understand speaking tasks, visualize the topic and language, practice and revise…

  While-speaking: understand others' words, activate schema, communicative strategies…

  Post-speaking: recall & reflect, improve & summarize…

- Students **apply** the above and prepare for class sharing:

  You will be interviewed in English, listen to the interview questions below and use proper thinking visualization tools to organize your ideas:

  Do you often see a doctor? Give your reasons.

  What do you do when you have a cold or a headache?

  Do you believe that "Happiness lies first of all in health"? Why or why not?

意图：学生通过课前微课导学，了解口语学习过程，即"说前—说中—说后"，以及每个阶段下面的具体策略；通过"学以致用"和"理解自查"任务尝试应用所学知识，检测对所学知识的理解，为课堂分享与讨论做好准备。

Do you buy health insurance? Give your reasons.

What do you think about the medical care in your university?

Watch the following video and analyze what communicative strategies did the interviewee use in her interview and write down your answers on your notebook.

Please choose one of the following topics to make a conversation with your classmates. After that, write down what you recall and reflect.

- Students **check** their personal understanding of the above and prepare for class **sharing**:

Why do we need to visualize the topic as well as the language to be used in the conversation?

After you visualize what you want to say, is it easier to speak out your ideas in English? If not, why?

How does schema help to improve your speaking skill?

Which of the pre-speaking, while-speaking and post-speaking strategies do you feel weakest in? And how do you plan to improve it?

While-class:

Step 1　Understanding and application: speaking learning strategies

Students **share** how they **apply and understand** the process of speaking learning and corresponding strategies. The teacher facilitates to organize discussion, explains, and supplements relevant information.

意图：通过学生微课任务分享及教师答疑和补充点评，帮助学生发现语言技能学习策略上存在的问题，构建正确理解，并形成良好的合作学习意识。

Step 2　Experience and application: speaking learning strategies

Students follow the procedure of speaking learning through different kinds of speaking tasks, experiences and **practice** the process step by step.

- Task 1: Prepared speaking task (1)

  (Unit 4　Warming-up *Watching, Listening and Speaking 1*)

  1. Students will be required to answer the questions in the warming-up part after they watch the video about the advertisement;

  2. Students could adopt the following tips in their oral practice.

意图：通过课堂体验应用，学生实训口语学习的过程，完整体验"说前—说中—说后"三大步骤。通过对常见的口语练习进行分类，帮助学生熟悉不同场景下的口语学习策略。

Listening
1. Analyze the task and predict the main ideas; underline key words; activate schema; use thinking maps to organize the structure of the text (definition, classification, list, cause and effect, compare and contrast, …)
2. Listen for the 1st time: arrange and adjust attention distribution; make notes; verify predictions
3. Listen for the 2nd time: edit and revise if there is any mistake

Speaking
1. Organize the structure of oral expressions according to notes; retrieve knowledge of the vocabulary and grammatical structure
2. Use synonyms
3. Practice and revise

有准备的口语表达包括根据听力材料直接回答相关问题（Task 1）、结合听力材料发表个人观点（Task 2）和围绕指定话题在规定时间内进行演讲（Task 3），无准备的口语表达即常见的情景对话（Task 4）。通过完成不同任务，学生能在实践中将听力过程及听力策略迁移到口语学习，并在归纳所使用的学习策略过程中进一步操练分类、列举、分析等思维技能。

- Task 2: Prepared speaking task (2)

  (Unit 4 Part *C Watching, Listening and Speaking 1*)

  1. Students will be required to express their own opinions after watching the video clip "College Diet" (e.g. Question 3);

  2. Students could adopt the following tips in their oral practice.

Listening
1. Analyze the task and predict the main ideas; underline key words; activate schema; use thinking maps to organize the structure of the text (definition, classification, list, cause and effect, compare and contrast, …)
2. Listen for the 1st time: arrange and adjust attention distribution; verify predictions; understand and summarize the main idea of the video clip in notes
3. Listen for the 2nd time: edit and revise if there is any mistake; add more details in each part
4. Reflect on the content to come up with one's own judgement/ confusion

Speaking
1. Activate schema; relate the task with one's own experiences with the help of the notes taken
2. Make a brief thinking map for speaking
3. Organize the structure of oral expressions according to the thinking map; retrieve knowledge of the vocabulary and grammatical structure

- Task 3: Prepared speaking task (3)
1. Students will be required to make a presentation/speech on a given topic (Topics can be related to previous tasks, e.g. about food or health, or topics from students' other courses.)
2. Students could adopt the following tips in their oral practice.

Speaking
1. Identify the theme and audience
2. Activate schema
3. Collect and organize related information
4. Make an outline for the speech (A thinking map can be adopted)
5. Write a draft and modify it
6. Familiarize with the draft and practice it with proper facial expressions

- Task 4: Unprepared speaking task
  (Unit 1 *Comprehensive English 1*, Handouts of IELTS Speaking Test Part 1/Part 3)
1. Students will be required to experience the conversation practice on the textbook/from the handout;
2. Students could adopt the following tips in their oral practice.

Listening
1. Retrieve knowledge of the vocabulary and grammatical structure to understand the given information
2. Analyze the conservation, especially if there is any implied meaning in communication

Speaking
1. Organize the structure of oral expressions according to notes; retrieve knowledge of the vocabulary and grammatical structure
2. Use synonyms
3. Practice and revise
4. Proper pauses and body language

Post-class:

Step 1   Summary and feedback

Students **summarize** what they have learned, thought, and argued for/against in the two periods and provide their **feedback**. Peers read and **comment** on the given feedback. —Speaking learning process

意图：学生通过总结、反馈和互评所学所思所疑，回顾口语学习过程，最大化掌握口语学习策略。

Step 2   Further practice

Students **design** their own speaking learning plan and refer to the textbook from their Speaking Lesson. They should follow their designed plan and **practice** the speaking learning process.

意图：学生在课后参考英语视听说课、英语口语课教材，或者相关专业课如综合英语的课堂学习内容，也可以结合听力实训打卡的内容，将听力与口语的话题结合起来，制定口语学习计划，进一步巩固口语学习策略，完成实训打卡任务。

X 课程优质教学设计

第一部分
《综合英语》

一、课程价值

（一）课程性质与目的

《综合英语》是高校英语专业基础阶段（一、二年级）的专业基础能力必修课，是进入高年级更高要求专业课程学习的先修课程。通过本课程学习，学生能够系统地掌握基础语言知识（语音、语法、词汇、篇章结构等），综合训练基本语言技能（听、说、读、写、译），逐步提高语篇阅读理解能力，了解英语各种文体的表达方式和特点，扩大词汇量和熟悉英语常用句型，具备基本的口头与笔头表达能力，提高运用英语进行交际的综合能力，为全面提高英语水平打好基础，达到英语专业本科语音，语法，词汇，听、说、读、写、译等各项指标的合格标准。

（二）教学理念与思路

《综合英语》作为"学习策略与思维训练"双融入 1+X+Y 特色课程体系中 X 课程——语言类课程的代表之一，与 1 课程《英语学习策略与思维训练》同期开设，通过任务型、探究式、项目式等多种教学方法，培养学生英语语言综合运用能力和思维能力，帮助学生养成良好学习习惯、形成正确情感态度和丰富社会文化知识，强调学生对目标知识学习和技能发展过程中的学习策略、思维过程、思维技能等的实践、应用与提升；教学全程为产出成果提供支架，重视过程性多元教学评价，开展评价标准的师生共建、评价过程的多方参与、评价结果的有效使用，强调评价技能的课程学习价值和人才培养价值。

（三）课程内容与任务

《综合英语》为序列课程，学分学时相对其他课程较高，平均每个学期完成 5～6 个单元的课程教学，课程目标、内容和重难点随着序列逐级提升。

《综合英语（3）》在《综合英语（1）》和《综合英语（2）》的基础上，继续扩充词汇量，通过练习使学生掌握话题相关的重点词汇，并能正确运用；继续加强听说训练，培养学生口头观点分析和表达能力；继续操练语法弱项，突出语法在交际中的实用功能；提高学生写作能力，重点掌握记叙文和说明文的写作方法和技巧；鼓励学生广泛阅读不同体裁的文章，正确理解文章意图，能对语篇的文体和修辞手法进行初步的赏析；指导学生运用翻译工具和策略，翻译复杂句式和修辞句，译文忠实原文，表达流畅；同时，在教学中注意训练学生的思维能力，充分利用信息化现代技术和手段，培养学生的自主学习能力。

二、教学案例

（一）设计理念

"Why Historians Disagree" 为《现代大学英语精读 3（第二版）》第十一单元，主题是历史学家的工作意义和相互之间产生分歧的原因，极具启发性，能引发学生对历史研究的深层思考；文体为典型的说明文，文中运用了下定义、类比的写作手法，在已完成的举例、引用等说明文常用写作手法基础上，能进一步丰富说明文写作技巧。

单元教学设计拟从学生现有水平出发，以思维发展为导向，以形成性评价为抓手，为学生完成任务提供足够的语言支架、知识支架和思维支架，服务学生语言知识、语言能力、文化意识、情感态度、思维能力等的同步发展，具体教学目标和任务如下：

1. 单元教学目标

语言知识和技能：能从词、句、篇章层次理解、推断、赏析课文文本，能理解和运用与历史研究相关的词汇表达自己对历史研究工作的理解，能应用下定义、类比的写作手法进行说明文写作；

文化意识：能理解历史研究的意义以及历史学家存在观点分歧的原因，对比中西文化对于历史研究的态度；

情感态度：能认识到历史学家工作的价值以及历史研究对人类的重要意义；

思维能力：能运用思维策略和工具辅助语言学习。

2. 本单元用时为八课时，主要学习内容和任务如下：

课时 1：通过推测、讨论激活学生有关历史研究的已有知识，通过小组活动和教师讲授，在真实语境中认识、操练重点词汇，最后赏析中外文化中历史研究的引言，对比中外文化对历史研究的看法，从自己的角度评论历史研究的价值。

课时 2：课前，采用翻转课堂帮助学生根据检索到的课文背景信息，就文本特点进行推测，运用思维导图阐释文章结构；课中，学生分享和讨论课前成果，教师指导学生有意识地反思自己和他人的思维过程，帮助认识说明文的文体特点以及过渡句和主题句对文章结构的重要性，并进行总结、归纳和点评。

课时 3 ~ 5：通过课堂问答、排序、判断、翻译、讨论等课堂活动帮助学生从词、句、篇章三个层面理解、分析和欣赏文章，理解历史学家之间存在观点分歧的原因，体会历史研究的魅力。

　　课时 6：从课文中"历史"的具体定义出发，通过对各种例子的分析，归纳"下定义"写作手法的主要类型和功能，最后完成正式和非正式两种定义的写作任务，教师反馈指导。

　　课时 7：通过学生分析课文中"上课迟到"和"美国内战"原因的类比手法的运用，结合大量例子，引导学生分析、归纳"类比"写作手法的形式和功能；提供常见的类比句型，帮助学生完成从易到难的写作任务并反馈。

　　课时 8：课前，通过小组讨论，拟定单元任务的评价标准；课中，引导学生讨论和确定本单元任务的评价标准，开展师生评价实践。最后，师生整体回顾本单元学习内容并进行分析评价，获取的反馈用于指导下一步教与学。

课时	教学内容	单元任务
1	话题讨论 / 词汇	假定你是一名历史学系教授，写一封信向新生介绍历史学家的工作内容和意义，必须使用下定义和类比两种写作手法；200 字以上，一周内独立完成。
2	整体阅读：背景信息 / 文体分析 / 结构分析	
3~5	文章的理解与欣赏：词、句、篇章	
6~7	下定义、类比的写作手法	
8	单元任务的评价与反思	

（二）代表课例

Unit 11　Why Historians Disagree

Targets: Sophomores majoring in English education

Materials: Unit 11 Why Historians Disagree, *Contemporary College English 3*

Teaching Philosophy: Student-centered, thinking-oriented, assessment for learning

Durations: 8 periods

Procedure:

<u>**Period 1**</u>

Objectives:

By the end of the period, students will be able

Linguistic Objectives

to **understand** and **use** expressions about historians;

to **express** a personal understanding about historians' job;

Non-linguistic Objectives

to **cooperate** with group members to **search for, analyze** and **reorganize** information;

to **develop** an objective evaluation standard on the value of a historian's job;

to **realize** the value of the study of history.

Important/Difficult Point(s):

New understanding about historians and their job;

Analysis of quotes on the value of the study of history.

Materials and Resources:

Courseware

Computer and projector

Pre-class task:

Step 1　Background information

Students learn about the background information about the essay like the author, theme, potential readers and its time background to **activate** related theme-based **schemas**, develop a further understanding for the background knowledge, and get ready for the new input.

意图：学生课前自主学习，激活已有与主题相关旧知，为新知输入做好铺垫。

Step 2　"Shark Attack"

- Students in three groups guess a letter in turn, which may be from the given word "archeologist". When they get the right letter, the teacher writes it down. Otherwise, they lose one point. At last, when the word "archeologist" is finished, the group who has got the most letters wins.

as example:

_____ (archeologist)

- The teacher asks questions to lead to the key word—historian, and then writes down the word "historian" on the blackboard.

An archeologist is a person who studies archaeology. How about people who study history?

意图：通过词汇游戏 "Shark Attack"，帮助学生激活历史考古旧知（activate schema），引入单元话题。

Step 3　Lead-in

- The teacher gives students a photo of a local historian (e.g. the curator of Chongqing Three Gorges Museum), and students **observe** and **figure out** his workplace and job responsibilities;
- Student representatives **share** their thoughts in class;
- The teacher **summarizes** and **supplements** the job of the person in the photo.

意图：学生基于照片观察和信息整合，盘活关于历史学家工作场地和工作职责的已有主题图式和语言图式，并进行小组分享；教师在对小组分享进行点评和引导的基础上进行主题知识补充和语言表达补充。

Step 4　Language building

- Students **match** a series of pictures to historians' job descriptions.

Gather historical data from various sources, including archives, books, and artifacts.

They engage with the public through educational programs and presentations.

They write reports, articles, and books on findings and theories.

They analyze and interpret historical information to determine its authenticity and significance.

They preserve and restore artifacts in museums and historic sites.

Trace historical developments in a particular field.

意图：通过图文匹配，帮助学生在真实语境和任务中学习主题词汇的形和义，了解历史学家工作范畴。

- Students use the given list of new words to **clarify** their own understanding about historians' job in groups.

Example:

Historians' job is very _____. They…

A list of new words:

immerse	discover	bring together	gather
study	analyze	trace	interpret
preserve	memorize	restore	dig
investigate	probe	revise	evidence
folk tale	manuscript	document	inscription
historical	development	archive	relics
event	skeleton	picture	sculpture
statistic	facts		

意图：学生运用所给词汇，就主题信息、观点和情感进行表达与交流，将词汇学习和日常交际联系起来。

- Students **discuss** and **present** their understanding of the significance of historians' job through **analysis** of western and Chinese views on the study of history.

Example: What is the purpose of studying history?

Histories make men wise; poets witty; the mathematics subtle; natural philosophy deep; moral grave; logic and rhetoric able to contend.

> —Francis Bacon(essayist) (1561—1626)

Those who cannot remember the past are condemned to repeat it.

> —George Santayan(philosopher) (1863—1952)

Take copper as a mirror, we can tidy up clothes; Take people as a mirror, we will know what we do is right or not; Take history as a mirror, we will know how the things rise and fall.

—Li Shimin(AD 559 —649)

稽其兴、坏、成、败之理。

> —— 司马迁（B.C.135—86）

意图：学生通过分析和讨论中西名人关于历史研究的名句，形成对历史研究价值的理解和评价，并进行分享与交流。

Period 2

Objectives:

By the end of the period, students will be able

Linguistic Objectives

to **develop** the reading strategy of **scanning**;

to **analyze** the text structure, genre and writing style;

Non-linguistic Objectives

to **retrieve** information and make reasonable prediction;

to **evaluate** other's analysis of the structure.

Important/Difficult Point(s):

Genre analysis

Structure analysis

Materials and Resources:

Courseware

Computer and projector

Pre-class task:

Students **analyze** the structure of the text and draw **mind tools** according to their understanding.

意图：训练学生自主分析文章结构，并用图形辅助呈现自己的理解。

Procedures:

Step 1   Global reading

- Students answer questions about the background information and **predict** the writing style of the essay.

  Example:

  Where could you probably find this article?

  Who is the author and who could be its potential readers?

  What is the article mainly about?

  What is the type of essay?

  Can you expect the stylistic feature of this writing?

- The teacher guides students to **analyze** the background information and the stylistic features.

意图：学生通过检索获取相关信息，分析文章作者和读者身份以及时代背景，推测文章文体特点。

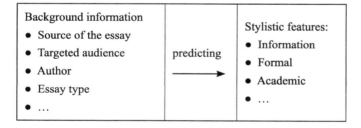

Step 2   Structure analysis

- Students **vote** for the best structure on Lan Mo app and the most popular students present their understanding of the structure.
- Students **comment** on their structure analysis.
- The teacher guides students to **locate** topic sentences and the transitions between paragraphs and then **analyze** the structure.
- Students **share adjustments** to their own mind map and the teacher **highlights** the functions of transitions.

意图：学生借助过渡语句和主题句帮助分析文章结构，并通过思维导图工具（树形图）进行呈现；学生能够客观评价他人的表现，同时，有意识地反思自己和他人的思维过程。

Step 3　Transitions

- The teacher **highlights** the functions of transitions between paragraphs by **analyzing** the transitions from Paras. 4, 6, 7, 11, 12.

意图：帮助学生意识到段落之间的衔接对理解整个文章框架的重要性。

Step 4　Assignment

The students preview the text in details and share their difficulties on Lan Mo App.

Periods 3-5

Objectives:

By the end of the periods, students will be able

Linguistic Objectives

to **understand** the definition of history, what historians do and why they disagree;

to **appreciate** the text in terms of its key expressions, involved sentences and writing style;

Non-linguistic Objectives

to **realize** the value of history study.

Important/Difficult Point(s):

The reasons why historians disagree;

Long and involved sentences.

Materials and Resources:

Courseware

Computer and projector

Step 1　Part 1　Introduction (Paras. 1—3)

- The teacher asks guiding **questions** to help the students **relate** to their own experiences and better **understand** the opening paragraphs.

  Example:

  How does the author begin? Is it a good beginning?

  How was history taught in your high school? What were you usually required to do? How were you evaluated? How about students in America?

  What are the common misconceptions about the study of history?

  Example:

意图：用问答和填写表格的形式帮助学生回忆历史学习经历，归纳段落大意，并厘清关于历史研究的谜思。

Misconceptions about the study of history	Can it explain the disagreement of historians?	Why?
A matter of memorizing "facts"	No	One is right while the other is wrong because of wrong facts; This is seldom the case.
A matter of choosing one good interpretation from among many	No	People feel two opposed points of view about an event, but they cannot both be right; People lack the ability to decide between them.

- Students work together to **analyze** and **understand** difficult sentences.

  Example:

  Most students are usually introduced to the study of history by way of a fat textbook and become quickly immersed in a vast sea of names, dates, events and statistics.

  Analyze the grammatical structure;

  Appreciate the use of "fat" and "immersed";

  Paraphrase and translate the sentence.

意图：帮助学生从用词汇、句子层面去理解、欣赏文本。

Step 2　Part II　Body (Paras. 4—12)

Reason 1 (Paras. 4—5): Historians cannot know everything because not everything was recorded.

Reason 2 (Para. 6) Historians select records they deem most significant.

Reason 3 (Paras. 7—10) Historians disagree because they begin from different premises.

Reason 4 (Para. 11) Analysis of different levels of cause and effect.

Reason 5 (Para. 12) Historians are often revising themselves.

- The teacher asks guiding **question**s to help the students **understand** how the author develops the logic line.
  Example:
  What methods dose the author use to **explain** his points?
  What's the example?
  Which of the following facts is **relevant** to the American entry into WWI? List them in **order** of descending importance.

> The sinking of American merchant ships by German submarines
> President Wilson's dissatisfaction with a new hat he bought during Jan., 1917
> British government's propaganda to win public support in America
> American bankers' large loans to the British
> Interception of the "Zimmermann Note"
> American political leaders' concern over the balance of power in Europe

What are the **interpretations** of these facts of the three groups?

> **First group:** These are the only important ones and they are equally important;
> **Second group:** The list is incomplete—leaving out facts like Wilson's pro—British attitude;
> **Third group:** These are not of equal importance—bankers' influence is the most important.

Is it true that in analyzing causes of historical events the further back one traces, the better?

意图：用问答、排序、是非判断等形式帮助学生分析作者的写作思路以及论证方法，并运用作者观点进行判断。

- Students work together to **analyze** and **understand** difficult sentences.

  Example:

  It would go something like this: National leaders contemplating war are more likely to be influenced by belligerent acts against countries than by their unhappiness with their haberdashers.

  Analyze the grammatical structure;

  Appreciate the use of "contemplating" and "belligerent";

  Paraphrase and translate the sentence.

意图：帮助学生从词汇、句子层面理解、欣赏文本。

Step 3　Part III　Conclusion (Para. 13)

- The teacher asks guiding **questions** to help the students **understand** how the author concludes.

  Example:

  Can we eliminate all disagreements? **Why not**?

  Why is it important to know why historians disagree?

  Why do the authors say being able to see truth as "an elusive yet intriguing goal in a never-ending quest" will make students appreciate the study of history?

意图：用问答形式帮助学生理解历史观点出现分歧的不可避免性，从而产生对历史研究的兴趣。

- Students work together to **analyze** and **understand** difficult sentences.

  Example:

  If the state of our knowledge were such that it provided us with a model of unquestioned validity that completely explained human behavior, we can. (Para. 13)

  Analyze the grammatical structure;

  Appreciate the use of "such";

  Paraphrase and translate the sentence.

意图：帮助学生从词汇、句子层面去理解、欣赏文本。

Step 4　Post-reading

- What do you **think** of the study of history now?
- The title of the text is "Why Historians Disagree." Do you think that the analyses only apply to historians? **Why** do people disagree in general?

意图：学生表达对历史学家之间产生观点分歧的看法，体会历史研究的魅力，并将历史学家产生观点分歧的原因延伸应用到生活中的其他方面。

Period 6

Objectives:

By the end of the period, students will be able

Linguistic Objectives

to **know** the types and functions of **definition**;

to **give definition** correctly and effectively in real writing;

Important/Difficult Point(s):

The **differences** between formal and informal definitions;

The use of definitions in real writing.

Materials and Resources:

Courseware

Computer and projector

Procedures:

Step 1　The definition of history

- The teacher helps the students **understand the definitions** of history and why definitions are given in the text.

  Example:

  What are the three definitions of history?

  in the broadest sense: the whole of the human past

  in a restricted sense: the recorded part of human life

  in a common sense: what historians write about the past

  Is it necessary here to define "history"?

  In what circumstances is definition necessary?

意图：问题从具体到一般层层递进，帮助学生从课文中"历史"的具体定义，思考"下定义"写作手法的功能。

Step 2　The types of definition

- The teacher gives the students a list of definitions and asks them to **categorize** them in any way that makes sense.
- The teacher gives clues to help the students **come up with** the two major types.

意图：鼓励学生发挥创造性思维，给各种定义归类。

Step 3　Formal definition

- The students are exposed to examples of formal definitions and **discuss** the form of each example.
- The students **sum up** the three elements of a formal definition: term, class and differentiating characteristics.
- The students **analyze** the three elements of given definitions in each example.
- The teacher draws the students' attention to expressions used to give a definition and asks the students to **apply** them to define "dentist" and "Zongzi".

意图：帮助学生通过例子中发现和归纳一般规律，并将一般规律运用于具体的写作中。

Step 4　Informal definitions

- The students **explore** the function and features of an informal definition through 10 informal definitions of "happiness".
- The students are exposed to more examples and **sum up** the methods used to give informal definitions.
- The students **practice** writing an informal definition for "love".
- Students and the teacher **comment** on selected definitions.

意图：鼓励学生欣赏含义隽永的十条对幸福的定义，体会非正式定义的特点和魅力，并通过例子发现和归纳非正式定义的写作方法，将之运用到具体的写作中，最后，对自己和他人的定义进行评价。

Period 7

Objectives:

By the end of the period, students will be able

Linguistic Objectives

to **know** the definition and functions of **analogy**;

to make correct and effective analogy in real writing;

Important/Difficult Point(s):

The understanding of analogy;

The use of analogy in real writing.

Materials and Resources:

Courseware

Computer and projector

Procedures:

Step 1　The definition of an analogy

- The teacher helps the students **understand** the use of analogy and **why** analogy is given in the text.
  Example:
  In Paragraph 11, what method dose the author use to **explain** his point ?
  Is it necessary to **illustrate** the cause of the Civil War with an analogy?
  In what circumstances is analogy necessary?
- The teacher helps the students give a definition to analogy.

意图：问题从具体到一般层层递进，帮助学生从课文中"上课迟到"和"美国内战"原因的类比，思考"类比"写作手法的定义。

Why are you late?	The cause of the Civil War
—overslept	—open fire at Fort Sumter
—I stayed up cramming for the exam.	—slavery
—I missed too many classes.	—the Compromise of 1850
—I didn't like the class.	—the militant abolitionist movement
—…	—the Missouri Compromise
	—the conflict over slavery in the constitutional convention
	—introduction of blacks to America in 1619

Step 2   Functions of an analogy

The teacher gives the students **examples** of analogy in everyday speech and literature and asks them to **summarize** the functions of an analogy.

Example:

a. Analogies in everyday speech

The structure of an atom is like a solar system. The nucleus is the sun, and electrons are the planets revolving around their sun.

b. Analogies in literature

The white mares of the moon rush along the sky beating their golden hoofs upon the glass Heavens.

c. Functions of analogies

To link an unfamiliar or a new idea with common and familiar objects. This makes it easier for readers to comprehend a new idea, which may have been difficult for them to understand otherwise.

To catch the attention of their readers. Analogies help increase readers' interest as analogies help them relate what they read to their life.

意图：帮助学生通过例子分析类比的具体运用，并从中归纳类比的功能。

Step 3   Patterns of an analogy

The teacher gives the students comment expressions for the writing of an analogy and **practice**.

Example:

A is to B as C is to D.

A to B is what C is to D.

(just) as A…B, (so) C…D.

If A were B, C would be D.

A is to B the same way as C is to D.

Practice:

Youths are to a society the same way as new cells are to a _____.

If love were what the rose is, I would like be like the _____.

Appropriate praise to a child is what the sun is to a _____.

意图：提供常见的类比句型，帮助学生运用所学知识完成练习。

Step 4　Assignment

What is it like to be a historian?

The students **write** an analogy for the job of historians in their unit task.

Period 8　Assessment and Feedback on the Unit Task

Objectives:

By the end of the period, students will be able

Linguistic Objectives

to **establish** the rubrics for the unit task;

to be able to **evaluate** their own and others' writing;

Important/Difficult Point(s):

The understanding of the rubrics;

The assessment practice.

Materials and Resources:

Courseware

Computer and projector

Step 1　Establishment of the rubrics

- Students in groups **come up with** the key points that should be included in the rubrics and explain why.
- The teacher guides the students to **construct** the rubrics in terms of contents, writing techniques and languages for the unit task.

  Example:

  Contents 内容

  All information is important to understanding the topic. 所有信息均与主题相关。(　　)

  It introduces historians' work clearly. 清楚介绍了历史学家的工作。(　　)

  It conveys personal understanding of the value of history study. 传达了作者对历史研究价值的个人的理解。(　　)

  Writing techniques 写作方法

  definition 下定义

意图：师生共建评价标准。

The definition has three key elements: term, class, and differentiating characteristics. 该定义包含三大关键要素。（   ）

The definition helps clarify the meaning of the term. 该定义有助于澄清概念。（   ）

Analogy 类比

The two things share several common qualities. 两者之间有共同点。（   ）

The analogy helps explain the writer's idea. 该类比有助于解释作者的想法。（   ）

Language 语言

Use specific words and phrases accurately to create a clear understanding of historians' work. 正确使用具体词汇和短语以介绍历史学家的工作。（   ）

Use correct grammar. 语法正确。（   ）

Step 2　Assessment of samples

- The students **evaluate** 2 samples given by the teacher and **justify** their decisions.
- The teacher elaborates on the rubrics based on the practice and makes sure that all students share the same understanding of the rubrics.

意图：师生共同进行评价实践，统一评价标准。

Assignment

Suppose you are a historian professor in our college, write a letter to the freshmen to introduce the job of a historian and its value. You should use a definition and an analogy to help them understand better. Over 200 words. Within one week.

假定你是一名历史学系教授，写一封信向新生介绍历史学家工作的内容和价值，必须使用下定义和类比两种写作手法。200 字以上，一周内独立完成。

附：

《现代大学英语精读 3（第二版）》（外语教学与研究出版社，杨立民主编）第 11 单元文章：

Unit 11 Why Historians Disagree
Allen F. Davis & Harold D. Woodman

1　Most students are usually introduced to the study of history by way of a fat textbook and become quickly immersed in a vast sea of names, dates, events and statistics. The students' skills are then tested by examinations that require them to show how much of the data they remember; the more they remember, the higher their grades. From this experience a number of conclusions seem obvious: the study of history is the study of "facts" about the past; the more "facts" you know, the better you are as a student of history. The professional historian is simply one who brings together a very large number of "facts". Therefore, students often become confused upon discovering that historians often disagree sharply even when they are dealing with the same event.

2　Their common-sense reaction to this state of affairs is to conclude that one historian is right while the other is wrong. And presumably, historians who are wrong will have their "facts" wrong. This is seldom the case, however. Historians usually all argue reasonably and persuasively. And, the "facts" —the names, dates, events, statistics— usually turn out to be correct. Moreover, they often find that contending historians more or less agree on the facts; that is, they use much the same data. They come to different conclusions because they view the past from a different perspective. History, which seemed to be a cut-and-dried matter of memorizing "facts", now becomes a matter of choosing one good interpretation from among many. Historical truth becomes a matter of personal preference.

3　This position is hardly satisfying. They cannot help but feel that two diametrically opposed points of view about an event cannot both be right; yet they lack the ability to decide between them.

4　To understand why historians disagree, students must consider a problem they have more or less taken for granted. They must ask themselves what history really is.

5　In its broadest sense, history denotes the whole of the human past. More restricted is the notion that history is the recorded past, that is, that part of human life which has left some sort of record such as folk tales, artifacts, or written documents. Finally, history may be defined as that which historians write about the past. Of course the three meanings are related. Historians must base their accounts on the remains of the past, left by people. Obviously they cannot know everything for the simple reason that not every event, every happening, was fully and completely recorded. Therefore the historian can only approximate history at best. No one can ever claim to have concluded the quest.

6 But this does not say enough. If historians cannot know everything because not everything was recorded, neither do they use all the records that are available to them. Rather, they select only those records they deem most significant. Moreover, they also re-create parts of the past. Like detectives, they piece together evidence to fill in the gaps in the available records.

7 Historians are able to select and create evidence by using some theory of human motivations and behavior. Sometimes this appears to be easy, requiring very little sophistication and subtlety. Thus, for example, historians investigating America's entry into World War I would probably find that the sinking of American merchant ships on the high seas by German submarines was relevant to their discussion. At the same time, they would most likely not use evidence that President Woodrow Wilson was dissatisfied with a new hat he bought during the first months of 1917. The choice as to which fact to use is based on a theory—admittedly, in this case a rather crude theory, but a theory nonetheless. It would go something like this: National leaders contemplating war are more likely to be influenced by belligerent acts against their countries than by their unhappiness with their haberdashers.

8 If the choices were as simple as this, the problem would be easily resolved. But the choices were not so easy to make. Historians investigating the United States' entry into World War I will find in addition to German submarine warfare a whole series of other facts that could be relevant to the event under study. For instance, they will find that the British government had a propaganda machine at work in the United States that did its best to win public support for the British cause. They will discover that American bankers had made large loans to the British, loans that would not be repaid in the event of a British defeat. They will read of the interception of the "Zimmerman Note," in which the German Foreign Secretary ordered the German minister in Mexico, in the event of war, to suggest an alliance between Germany and Mexico whereby Mexico, with German support, could win back territory taken from Mexico by the United States in the Mexican War. They will also find among many American political leaders a deep concern over the balance of power in Europe, a balance that would be destroyed—to America's disadvantage—if the Germans were able to defeat the French and the British and thereby emerge as the sole major power in Europe.

9　What then are historians to make of these facts? One group could simply list them. By doing so, they would be making two important assumptions: (1) those facts they put on their list are the main reasons, while those they do not list are not important; and (2) those things they put on their list are of equal importance in explaining the U. S. role. But another group of historians might argue that the list is incomplete in that it does not take into account the generally pro-British views of Woodrow Wilson, views that stemmed from the President's background and education. The result will be a disagreement among the historians. Moreover, because the second group raise the question of Wilson's views, they will find a number of relevant facts that the first group would ignore. They will concern themselves with Wilson's education, the influence of his teachers, the books he read, and the books he wrote. In short, although both groups of historians are dealing with the same subject they will come to different conclusions and use different facts to support their points of view. The facts selected, and those ignored, will depend not on the problem studied but on the points of view of the historians.

10　Similarly a third group of historians might maintain that the various items on the list should not be given equal weight, that one of the reasons listed, say, bankers' loans, was most important. The theory here would be that economic matters are the key to human motivation, and that a small number of wealthy bankers have a disproportionate ability to influence government.

11　In the examples given, historians disagree because they begin from different premises. But there is still another realm of disagreement which stems from something rather different. Historians sometimes disagree because they are not really discussing the same thing. Often they are merely considering different levels of cause and effect. Suppose the teacher asked you "Why were you late for class this morning?" "I was late for class, "you explained, "because I overslept." Or to use a historical example, "The Civil War began because South Carolina shore batteries opened fire on the federal garrison at Fort Sumter on April 12, 1861." Neither statement can be faulted on the grounds that it is inaccurate; at the same time, however, neither is sufficient as an explanation of the event being considered. The next question is obvious: Why did you oversleep, or why did relations between one state and the Federal government reach the point where differences had to be settled by war? In other words, we have to go beyond the proximate cause and probe further and further. But as we dig more deeply into the problem, the answer becomes more difficult and complex. In the end, you might argue that the ultimate cause of your being late was the fact that you were born, but obviously this goes too far back to be meaningful. That you were born is of course a necessary factor, but it is not a sufficient factor; it does not really tell enough to explain your behavior today. Similarly, you could trace the cause of the Civil War back to the discovery of America, but again, that is a necessary but not a sufficient cause. The point at which causes are both necessary and sufficient is not self-evident. Therefore, historians may again disagree about where to begin the analysis. By now students should see that the well-used phrase "let the facts speak for themselves" has no real meaning. The facts do not speak for themselves; historians use the facts in a particular way and therefore they, and not the facts, are doing the speaking.

12 Historians not only often disagree with others. They often disagree with themselves. Indeed, they are often revising their ideas. They have to do so because they are constantly discovering new information, gaining new insights from other social scientists and mastering and using new techniques. Historian also learn from each other and benefit from international comparisons of similar events and institutions.

13 Can we eliminate all disagreement? If the state of our knowledge were such that it provided us with a model of unquestioned validity that completely explained human behavior, we can. But since we do not have such a complete and foolproof explanation, disagreements are destined to remain. When students realize that there is no one easy answer to the problems historians raise and that "truth" is but an elusive yet intriguing goal in a never-ending quest, they will find the study of history to be a significant, exhilarating, and useful part of their education.

第二部分
《英语视听说》

一、课程价值

（一）课程性质与目的

《英语视听说》是普通高等院校英语专业学生基础阶段（一、二年级）开设的一门专业基础能力必修课。通过本课程的学习，学生能够了解英语听力技能发展基本规律，应用英语听力技能学习策略和思维技能，扩展各类话题语言储备，提高英语听力理解综合能力；能够了解英语口语技能发展基本规律，应用英语口头表达学习策略与思维技能，形成地道的英语口语表达，有效进行跨文化沟通，做到语音语调自然、语言表达得体、有思想，为后续英语专业学习奠定良好的基础。

（二）课程理念与思路

《英语视听说》作为"学习策略与思维训练"双融入1+X+Y特色课程体系中X课程——语言类课程的代表之一，与1课程《英语学习策略与思维训练》同期开始开设，提供机会帮助学生基于《英语学习策略与思维训练》课程中听学英语听力和口语技能发展策略和思维技能训练理论与实践，采用任务型教学法，在课内外视听说技能培养中融入相关思维训练，半显性化学习策略与思维技能训练，促进学生英语听力技能、口语表达和思维能力的同步提升。

（三）课程内容与任务

《英语视听说》为序列课程，分为《英语视听说（1）》《英语视听说（2）》《英语视听说（3）》和《英语视听说（4）》4个序列。其中《英语视听说（1）》主要针对英语简短对话、长对话及篇章听力技能，旨在掌握相关场景的关键语句以及常用英语语音缩略语形式；《英语视听说（2）》继续针对英语简短对话、长对话及语篇中的相关场景的关键语句和文体特点进行训练，培养学生捕捉细节的能力，在语音方面使学生养成连读、不完全爆破的意识；

《英语视听说（3）》主要针对英语短对话、小短文及微型讲座等方面的听力技巧，让学生熟悉以上几种听力体裁的文体特点和表达句式，掌握英文速记的方法；《英语视听说（4）》主要针对较大难度的英语长对话、篇章、微型讲座及新闻语篇听力的听力技巧，掌握有效获取听力文本信息的能力，提高英文速记效率，能就日常英文话题做到流利表达。

二、教学案例

（一）设计理念

《新世纪师范英语系列教材视听说教程3》第3单元的主题是太空探索。绝大多数学生对这一话题不熟悉，知识储备也相对较少，但该话题与人类社会发展关系密切，可利用大量的相关资源作为信息输入，激发学生的学习兴趣、求知欲和探索欲。

本单元共计4个学时，旨在综合训练学生的捕捉信息、排序、分类等技能，重点训练学生的逻辑分析和批判思维能力。通过本单元的综合训练，学生能够理解太空探索的原因和利弊，并提升逻辑分析和批判性思维能力。

本单元各个学时的教学内容及教学任务见下表：

课时	教学内容	教学任务
1	话题引入 听力1：中国太空项目	识别飞行器 了解中国的太空项目 根据听力材料进行细节捕捉、判断和推理
2	听力2：猎户座太空任务 小组讨论：为什么进行太空探索	了解美国的猎户座太空飞行任务 根据听力材料进行综合分析、判断 结合听力1和听力2材料分析太空探索的原因
3	听力3：科技能解决我们的难题吗？ 小组讨论、辩论	讨论科技对人们生活的影响 分析讨论太空探索的利弊 讨论太空探索对人类的影响
4	技能训练：识别因果关系	学习使用鱼骨图分析事件的因果关系 结合鱼骨图复述本单元的主题

（二）代表课例

Unit 3　Space Exploration

Targets: Sophomores majoring in English education

Materials: Unit 3 Space Exploration, *Viewing, Listening and Speaking, Student's Book 3*

Teaching Philosophy: Task-based, thinking-oriented

Durations: 4 periods

Unit objectives:

By the end of the unit, students will be able to

Linguistic objectives

to **know** about some useful expressions related to space and space exploration;

to **understand** space exploration through group discussion;

to **describe** the cause-effect relationship with the fish-bone diagram.

Non-linguistic objectives

to **know** about China's space station program;

to **develop** thinking skills of **analysis, judgment** and reasoning.

Procedure:

<u>**Period 1**</u>

Objectives:

By the end of the period, students will be able to

Linguistic objectives

to **know** about and **identify** some flying objects;

to **classify** China's space station program from the given video;

to **record and summarize** the missions for the spacecraft Tiangong;

to **analyze and judge** the details from the given video.

Non-linguistic objectives

to develop thinking skills of **remembering, understanding and analyzing**;

to develop the sense of national pride.

Important/Difficult Point(s):

Classify Tiangong missions of China's space program;

Analyze details from the video clip of the unit.

Materials and Resources:

Video

Mp3

Courseware

Computer and projector

Procedure:

Step 1   Pre-listening activities

- Lead-in: Pair work

  Describing the picture—What can you see in the picture?

  The teacher shows the picture of space to the students, and asks them to figure out what they can see in the picture to introduce the topic of the unit.

意图：两位同学讨论图片内容，通过描述图片引出本单元主题，激活已有信息，提取本单元关键词。通过比较地球与外太空的不同，训练学生的分析能力，并为后面太空探索的讨论打下基础。

Is outer space as same as our earth? If not, what are the differences between them?

Earth   differences?   **outer space**

                                          no air

                                          …

- Look and identify: look at the pictures and **identify** the flying objects.

  Students discuss the pictures of flying objects in the textbook and try to identify each of them to be further familiar with the topic discussed in the unit.

意图：通过小组讨论和观察，识别图片中的飞行器，利用观察到的飞行器特征来推断该飞行器的类别，由此补充航天器相关知识，为后续听力材料的理解做铺垫。

Step 2　While-listening activities: China's Space Station Program

- **First-time playing: watch and classify**

The teacher plays the video about China's space station program for the first time and requires students to identify the 3 phases of China's space station program. Take down notes of the key points of each phase. Fill in the following table based on the notes.

Space station program	
Phase 1	
Phase 2	
Phase 3	

意图：教师播放视频，要求学生识别出中国太空计划的 3 个阶段，并记录每个阶段的关键信息，在信息记录的基础上完成表格，训练学生理解、识别和分类的思维能力。

A. launching Shenzhou-5　　B. launching Shenzhou-6

C. launching Shenzhou-7　　D. launching Shenzhou-8

E. launching Shenzhou-9　　F. launching Shenzhou-10

G. launching Tiangong Space Lab

H. constructing a space station

- **Second-time playing: focused listening: How can you summarize the missions for the spacecraft in the following table?** Watch the video, summarize and complete the table.

The teacher plays the video for the second time, and asks students to find out the detailed information for the launch of Tiangong spacecraft. Take down notes and fill in the following table.

意图：教师再次播放视频，在第二遍播放中激活学生捕捉到的已有信息，结合表格内容捕捉要点及关键词，并作简要概括，训练学生的分析和综合理解能力。

Tiangong—1	
Tiangong—2	
Tiangong—3	

● Third-time watching: Watch and **judge**

The teacher plays the video for the third time and requires students to pay much attention to some details and judge whether the following statements are true or false.

1. The docking of a manned space shuttle and a space lab is part of the second phase.

2. Astronauts of Shenzhou-6 performed extra-vehicular activities in space.

3. Shenzhou-8 is an unmanned spacecraft, while Shenzhou-9 and Shenzhou-10 are manned ones.

4. All the Tiangong Space Labs can have astronauts stationed inside.

5. New types of materials, vegetables and fruits will be developed in Tiangong 3.

意图：在前两遍播放视频的基础上，学生已基本理解视频的主要内容，教师第 3 次播放视频，让学生判断部分信息的正误，训练学生的理解、分析和判断能力。

Step 3　Post-listening activities

● Retell: **Retell** China's space program based on what you have watched.

The teacher asks students to retell the main points of China's space program based on the video. Students can retell it with the help of the former exercises, e.g. the 3 phases of China's space program, the launch of Tiangong spacecraft. Therefore, students can get to know more about China's space program.

意图：要求学生基于前面两遍的听力练习复述视频的主要信息，训练学生的理解和概括能力，通过复述使学生了解中国的太空计划，从而也唤起学生的民族自豪感。

● Group **discussion**: Why do man explore space? What difficulties may they meet? Draw a mind map to help you.

5—6 students make a group to discuss the reasons why human beings explore space based on what they have got and try to analyze and imagine difficulties in the space exploration.

意图：学生基于所看视频讨论太空探索的原因，结合前面的讨论分析太空探索可能会遇到的困难，训练学生的综合分析能力。要求学生使用思维导图来厘清思路。

Period 2

Objectives:

By the end of the period, students will be able

Linguistic objectives

to **know about** the Orion mission in the U.S.;

to **analyze** and **evaluate** the Orion mission;

to **evaluate** space exploration.

Non-linguistic objectives

to develop thinking skills of **analysis** and **evaluation**;

to develop their world outlook.

Important/Difficult Point(s):

Make evaluation on the Orion mission;

Make evaluation on space exploration.

Materials and Resources:

Video

Mp3

Courseware

Computer and projector

Procedure:

Step 1　Pre-listening activity

Lead-in question: Do you know anything about space program of other countries? How about the U.S.A.?

> In the last period, students have got to know China's space program. In this period, they are going to know something about the space program of the U.S. Students will exchange information before the whole-class discussion.

意图：通过提问唤起学生的旧知，引出本节课话题，做好相关语言准备。

Step 2   While-listening activities

- Watch and **describe**: Students watch the video clip and describe the steps of the Orion mission, and fill in the blanks.

  (1) launch   (2) spiral out to the moon
  (3) cruise to asteroid   (4) _____
  (5) _____   (6) return to lunar orbit
  (7) _____   (8)_____   (9) _____

意图：通过观看视频，学生记录猎户座任务的主要步骤，训练捕捉细节和信息提取的能力。在听前可让学生预览听力材料以对相关信息定位。

- Watch, **analyze** and **evaluate**: Students watch the video clip and answer the following questions:

  What do you think of the Orion mission?

  Which part do you think is the most difficult? why?

  How will the mission impact people's life?

意图：通过观看视频，训练学生在综合理解视频的基础上对猎户座任务进行分析和评价。同桌两人进行一问一答以交换信息。

Step 3   Post–listening activity: group discussion

- Based on the China's space station program and the Orion mission, what does space exploration bring to us?

  1. Draw a **mind map**

  Ask students to draw a mind map to help them have a clear structure and think about what benefits we can get from space exploration. Talk about their own opinion to their group members.

  2. Group presentation

  Each group will choose a speaker to present their opinion and share in class.

意图：通过前面对中国卫星发射和美国猎户座任务的了解，学生分组讨论太空探索对人类生活的影响，并借助思维导图表达观点，帮助梳理结构，培养分析和评价能力以及正确的世界观。

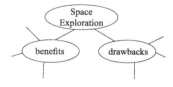

Assignment

Personal speaking: life on the moon

Based on what we have learned in these 2 periods, think about if one day, we moved to the moon, what would our life be? Collect some information from the Internet, talk to your roommates, and then record it to your mobile phone and upload it to QQ.

<u>Period 3</u>

Objectives:

By the end of the period, students will be able

Linguistic objectives

to **understand** space exploration fully;

to **analyze** pros and cons of space exploration;

to make a speech based on **mind maps**;

to have a **debate** on the given topic.

Non-linguistic objectives

to develop thinking skills of **understanding** and **analyzing**;

to develop critical thinking.

Important/Difficult Point(s):

Analyze pros and cons of space exploration;

Have a debate on the given topic.

Materials and Resources:

Video

Mp3

Courseware

Computer and projector

Procedure:

Step 1　Warm up: life on the moon

Invite some of the students to share their speaking in class.

意图：课前通过分享上次布置的课后作业进行热身，让学生迅速进入上课状态。

Step 2　Lead-in question: Can technology solve our big problems?

Based on what they have discussed in the first two periods, students may have some idea about the benefits of space exploration, but can all our big problems be solved by technology? They can discuss it with their peers.

意图：课前抛出主题问题供学生思考讨论，引出本课主题，做好语言准备。

Step 3　Listening practice: Can technology solve our big problems?

- Pre-watching: Identify the key words

  Before watching the video, ask students to circle the key words in each sequence to help them be familiar with the material.

意图：观看视频前学生通过圈出关键词预览材料，熟悉主题。

- While-watching

  1. Number the **order**: students watch a speech and number the points according to the sequence

意图：通过观看视频整理调整以下要点的顺序，填出关键信息，训练学生分析、排序、捕捉细节等技能。

(　) A. The Apollo program was just one among a series of triumphs.

(　) B. The reasons we can't solve big problems are more complicated and more profound.

(　) C. We used to solve big problems.

(　) D. President Kennedy gave the reason for going to the moon.

(　) E. Problems today seem intractably hard.

(　) F. The current technology doesn't solve humanity's big problems.

(　) G. The Apollo mission is an irreproducible model for the future.

(　) H. The four criteria must be met for a problem to have a technological solution.

2. Gap-filling

In this part, students will watch the video for 2 times, and then they will fill in the blanks in the following part. Sometimes, we can't solve big problems because A. _____. Today, less than two percent of the world's enemy consumption derives from advanced, renewable sources such as solar, wind and biofuels, less than two percent, and B. _____. Coal and natural gas are cheaper than solar and wind, and petroleum is cheaper than biofuels. We want alternative energy sources C. _____. None exists. Now, technologists, business leaders and economists all basically agree on D. _____ would spur the development of alternative energy; mostly, E. _____, and F. _____. But there's no hope in the present political climate that we will see the U.S. energy policy or international treaties that G. _____.

Sometimes, big problems that had seemed technological turned out not to be so. Famines were long understood to be caused H. _____. But 30 years of research have taught us that I. _____ that catastrophically affect food distribution. Technology can improve things like crop yields or systems for storing and transporting food, but there will be famines so long as J. _____.

- Post-watching

  Go back to the **question**: Can technology solve our big problems? **Why**?

  In this part, based on the video they have watched, students will reconsider the question and have a deeper understanding of space exploration and share their ideas with the class.

  Group discussion

  A picture shown in this speech is actually the cover of a 2012 issue of *MIT Technology Review*, with the face of Apollo astronaut Edwin Buzz Aldrin, then 82. How do you understand Aldrin's statement on the cover (You promised me Mars colonies? Instead, I got Facebook.)? Discuss with your partner this warning given by Aldrin.

意图：基于视频的输入，学生会重新思考之前提出的问题，训练学生的批判性思维能力和综合理解能力。

Step 4　Give a speech: The Benefits Space Exploration Brings about

- Draw a mind map.

意图：利用思维导图帮助学生理清思路、构建框架。

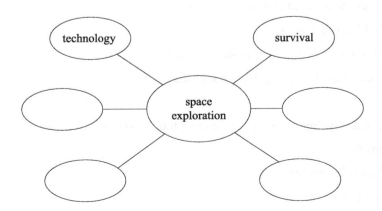

Students can firstly discuss with their partners, and then draw a mind map to help them have a better understanding and clear structure.

- Students make a **speech** based on the **mind map.**
  Students can make their speech by using the key words in the mind map, which will help them have a clear structure in their mind.

意图：学生依据思维导图组织语言表达，并在小组内分享。

Step 5　Debate: To Go or Not to Go?

- Group discussion.
  As can be seen, space exploration indeed can benefit a lot human beings, but it also requires time, money and resources. Do you think space exploration is really worthy? Discuss with your group members first and decide your opinion on to go or not to go.
- Have a **debate**.
  After students have expressed their ideas, they can be divided into two parts to debate the topic. Finally the teacher will give feedback to them.

意图：基于对前面太空探索优缺点的讨论，学生再次思考太空探索的可行性，并互相表达观点，最后形成辩论，进一步训练学生的批判性思维能力。

Period 4

Objectives:

By the end of the period, students will be able

Linguistic objectives

to **know** the cause-and-effect relationship and its significance;

to **identify** the cause-and-effect relationship;

to **apply** the fishbone diagram to analyze the cause-and-effect relationship;

to **express** causes and effects clearly by using the fishbone diagram;

Non-linguistic objectives

to develop thinking skills of **analyzing** by using the thinking tool—fishbone diagram.

Important/Difficult Point(s):

Identify the cause-and-effect relationship;

Apply the fishbone diagram to analyze causes and effects.

Materials and Resources:

Video

Mp3

Courseware

Computer and projector

Procedure:

Step 1　Skill focus: identifying the cause-and-effect relationship

- Knowing the skill: listen and **define**

  Students will get to know how to identify the cause-and-effect relationship through listening to the audio. And while they are listening, they should note down the key points which will help them understand fully.

  Cause-and-effect is a way of describing _____.

  Mary knocking over the soda can is the cause, and _____ is the effect.

  Something happens and we want to know why, so we search for _____. We also want to predict _____ if something were to happen in the future.

  意图：通过输入音频，帮助学生理解什么是因果关系，训练学生的听音定位能力和概括能力。

- **Draw** a cause-and-effect diagram

  Ask students to think about the reasons of car accidents and try to draw a fishbone to help them eastablish the cause-and-effct relationship.

  意图：通过分析原因，用因果关系鱼骨图帮助学生建立因果逻辑思维联系，为口语表达打基础。

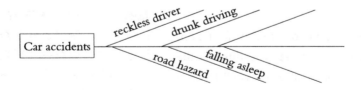

- Practicing the skill

  Identify the transitional words signifying the cause-and-effect relationship

  In this part, students will be required to identify the transitional words indicating causes and effects in the audio.

  Cause: because, due to…

  Effect: so, therefore…

  意图：通过播放音频，让学生在听力材料中识别出表示因果关系的连接词，帮助学生建立原因和结果的逻辑联系。

Apply the fishbone diagram to list the reasons why we can't solve big problems according to the speech given by Jason Pontin.

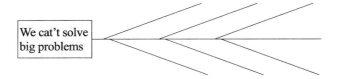

意图：让学生运用鱼骨图重新梳理之前讨论的科技不能帮我们解决大问题的话题，以进一步帮助学生厘清思路。

Step 2　Project Debate: Should we explore space?

● Should we spend money exploring space?
Draw a fishbone diagram
Express your idea
Debate
In this part, students will have a project debate based on all they have learned in this unit. They can do it step by step. In the first step, they can draw a fishbone diagram to help think about the reasons why human beings explore space, including both the pros and cons of it; in the second step, they can express their ideas based on the fishbone, and finally they will be divided into two groups and make a debate to have a clearer and better understanding of space exploration.

意图：基于本单元的听力文本输入和语言输入以及课前布置的小组项目调查，学生再次回到我们是否应该进行太空探索这一话题进行辩论，可借助鱼骨图帮助学生厘清思路，说明原因，学生展开辩论，对前面所有内容进行整合，回到本单元的主题，首尾呼应，训练学生综合理解、批判性思维和口头表达能力。

● **Assignment**
Suppose one day, you would go to outer space for travel, but you can only bring one item that you think is the most important for you. What is it? And why? Draw a fishbone diagram first, then express your idea based on the fishbone, record your reading by your mobile phone, and upload it.

意图：课后作业为本节课的延伸，继续使用鱼骨图帮助学生厘清思路并清晰表达原因和结果，同时训练学生的思维分析能力。

第三部分
《英语读写》

一、课程价值

（一）课程性质与目的

《英语读写》作为高校英语专业基础阶段（一、二年级）的一门专业基础能力必修课，旨在夯实学生对多种体裁的语篇阅读分析能力和写作能力，扩展学生对各类话题的语言储备，为高年级更高要求的专业课程的学习奠定基础。通过本课程的学习，学生能够基本具备文体意识和主要的文体知识，熟悉不同体裁的篇章特征，同时能够分类记忆涵盖政治、经济、文化、社会、科技、心理等多方面的词汇和句式。学生在此基础上掌握核心阅读和写作技能与策略，从而提升阅读速度，能够进行一定深度的分析阅读，并将通过阅读所掌握的知识（包括文体、学科、逻辑等）运用于同类体裁和话题的写作中。

（二）课程理念与思路

《英语读写》作为"学习策略与思维训练"双融入 1+X+Y 特色课程体系中 X 课程——语言类课程的代表之一，与 1 课程《英语学习策略与思维训练》同期开设，帮助学生基于《英语学习策略与思维训练》课程中听学英语阅读和写作技能发展策略和思维技能训练理论与实践；两学期课程整体采用 TOP-DOWN 的方式，基于图式理论，从篇章到字句，从行文布局和构思到语言质量的提升，半显性化学习策略与思维技能训练，促进学生英语阅读技能、写作能力和思维能力的同步提升。

（三）课程内容与任务

《英语读写》作为序列课程，分为《英语读写（1）》和《英语读写（2）》，主要包含四种基础文体的阅读与写作训练：描写文、记叙文、说明文和议论文。《英语读写（1）》着重通过阅读，让学生对不同文体有整体的认识，能够把握文体特征和文章结构，有整体行文布局意识，同时储备不同主题的文章图式，积累知识与语言，构建理性分析与评价的批判性思维范式，详见表1。《英语读写（2）》偏重写作训练，以读促写，引导学生将文体知识应用于写作中。教学重点从整体布局过渡到文段组织、词句语法等，并且强调批判性思维品质与能力的内化与迁移，详见表2。

表 1 《英语读写（1）》学习内容与学时分配

模块	教学内容	总学时	理论学时	实训学时
模块一	摘要和读书报告	8	0	8
模块二	描写文阅读与写作（侧重阅读）	8	2	6
模块三	记叙文阅读与写作（侧重阅读）	12	2	10
模块四	说明文阅读与写作（侧重阅读）	16	2	14
模块五	议论文阅读与写作（侧重阅读）	16	2	14
模块六	综合训练（侧重阅读）	8	0	8
合计		68	8	60

表 2 《英语读写（2）》学习内容与学时分配

模块	教学内容	总学时	理论学时	实训学时
模块一	描写文阅读与写作（侧重写作）	12	2	10
模块二	记叙文阅读与写作（侧重写作）	16	2	14
模块三	说明文阅读与写作（侧重写作）	20	2	18
模块四	议论文阅读与写作（侧重写作）	12	2	10
模块五	综合训练（侧重写作）	8	0	8
合计		68	8	60

二、教学案例

（一）设计理念

记叙文作为《英语读写（1）》的主要文体之一，与描写文有承接也有差异。记叙文阅读与写作共计 12 学时。本单元教学设计从"以读促识、以读促写、读写结合、策略运用、思维发展"的理念出发，确定整体教学目标如下：

（1）文体知识：学生能够理解并记忆记叙文的相关文体知识，在阅读中辨别其主要文体特征，并在写作中加以应用；能够归纳描写文和记叙文的相同点与不同点。

（2）阅读策略：学生能够根据阅读目的，合理分配注意力，运用注意力策略；能够根据首尾段推测写作目的和篇章大意；能够快速识别体现时间和空间的信号词及动词的时态变化，分析文章行文逻辑；能够区分描写与记叙的不同语言表达。

（3）写作策略：学生能够按照写前——写中——写后的基本流程，操练写前计划、写中调整、写后修改的元认知策略；能够在构思及写作过程中应用阅读所得的知识、信息和语言表达；能够理解并制定合理的写作标准，对同伴和自身写作进行批判性评价。

（4）批判性思维

学生能够在多样化的学习任务中发展批判性思维品质，如不轻易下结论，基于客观信息进行理性判断，有开放心态和同理心等；能够理解、应用并强化批判性分析与评价的高阶思维技能。

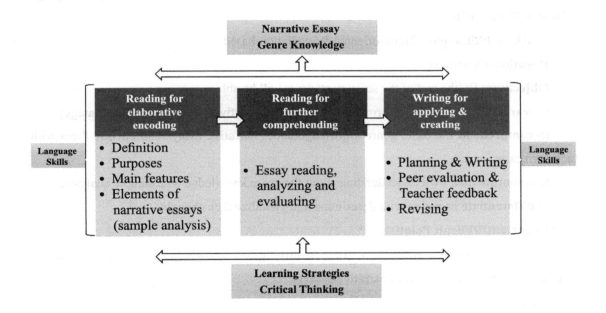

如上所示，本单元学习内容与任务主要包括精细编码阅读、深入阅读理解以及应用与创造性写作。精细编码阅读主要引导学生对记叙文文体的理论知识进行编码记忆，包括定义、目的、主要特征以及该文体的组成元素；在深入阅读理解部分，学生要应用文体知识对有关文章进一步分析和评价，夯实理论基础；在应用与创造性写作阶段，通过构思、写作、同伴评价和教师反馈、修改过程性写作训练，引导学生完成文体知识输入到输出的转化，提升写作沟通的能力。这三个阶段充分融合了英语读写技能、学习策略与批判性思维的训练，旨在加强学生对记叙文文体知识的理解、记忆和创造性运用。

（二）代表课例

English Reading and Writing
Narrative Essays（1）— Reading for elaborative encoding

Targets: Freshmen majoring in English education

Preparatory course: Learning Strategies and Thinking Skills, Comprehensive English

Parallel courses: Comprehensive English

Prior learning: Descriptive Essays

Materials: Unit 3 Narrative Essays, *English Writing P40—46*, Shanghai Foreign Language Education Press, 2016

Teaching Philosophy: Think-oriented & mediation-based

Durations: 4 periods

Objectives: By the end of the session, students will be able

to **search** for the targeted information by using the selective attention learning strategy;

to **comprehend** the basic genre knowledge about narrative essays and **encode** them with their own experience;

to **elaborate** their own understanding about the genre knowledge with sample analysis;

to **differentiate** narration with description and **visualize** their thoughts.

Important/Difficult Point(s):

Comprehending and encoding of the narrative genre knowledge: definition, purposes, common features and elements of narrative essays;

Sample analysis;

Comparison of narrative essays with descriptive essays.

Materials and Resources:

Courseware

Computer and projector

Procedure:

<u>**Period 1**</u>

Step 1　Activation and lead-in

Students put up their hands if they have experienced the following situations:

You were **complaining** to your friends about your awful day;

Your parents were **telling** you how they met or fell in love with each other;

Seniors from your university were **sharing their experience** of making full use of your college time, joining clubs or taking part-time jobs;

You were **explaining** the most incredible **moments** about the past NBA match to your teammate;

You were reading **a novel or a story**, and sometimes laughing, sometimes feeling sad or even crying.

The teacher counts the numbers of students for each questions, introduces the concept of narration to the whole class, and then guides the whole class to discuss the purposes of narration in each situation.

意图：通过生活场景的回忆，激活学生跟记叙文有关的图式，引入单元主题。

Step 2　Information searching and elaborative encoding

Students read Part One (Page 40—41) in the textbook and **search** for targeted information about the below questions:

What is narration?

What are the purposes of narrative essays?

What are the main features of narrative essays?

The teacher instructs students to circle key words of each question and identify them in the textbook first. Meanwhile, students are reminded of searching for targeted information in the matching part and underline key words of the answers. Selective attention learning strategies are introduced and stressed here.

意图：帮助学生带着目的进行阅读，充分运用选择性注意策略抓取关键信息。

Students form groups of 3—4 and **explain** their understanding about these questions. Students give examples of their own experiences to **illustrate** their thoughts.

The teacher invites 2 groups for each question to **share** their ideas. Other groups can add more ideas if they have different thoughts.

意图：通过讨论形成自身对于以上概念和知识点的理解，并关联自身经历进行精细编码，加强记忆。

Period 2

Step 1　Skimming

The teacher leads students to find "Introduction, Body and Conclusion", the three parts in the textbook from page 41—46. Students work in groups and **search** for key words answering the question:

What should be included in each part?

Then each group needs to **skim** the textbook, **imitate** the mind-map below and **draw** one for "Elements of Narrative Essays".

意图：再次让学生操练选择性注意策略跳读课本，挑选关键信息，并通过思维导图进行分类整理，让学生对于记叙文写作要素有整体认知。同时，引导学生运用元认知策略反思和分享小组合作过程的学习方法。

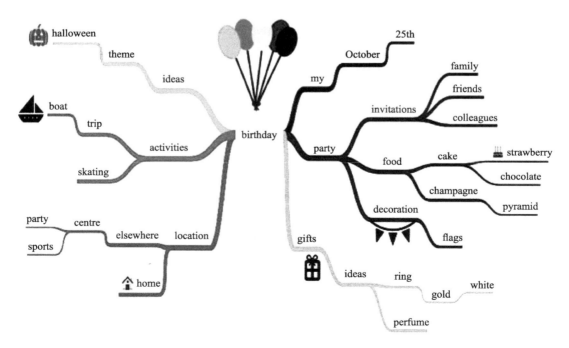

Students can start from

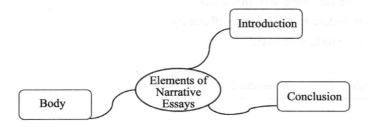

Each group **shares** their work in the Lan Mo app and **revise** their own one.

2 groups are invited to **share** how they find the answers and design their work.

Step 2　Sample analysis for Introduction

The teacher guides students to analyze Sample 1 on page 41 by asking them to **underline** the key words to show:

When—Easter

Where—our front yard

Who—Gillion, I 7/20

What—fourth egg hunt, the day, I received my most memorable gift.

Point of view-first person

Then the teacher leads the whole class to **discuss** what can be the thesis statement and write the purpose of this essay.

Then students **apply** the same way to analyze Sample 2.

When—?

Where—?

Who—I

What—hardest thing, learning how to swim

Point of view—first person

意图：强化抓取关键信息的阅读策略，并通过两个案例的比较分析，归纳、总结 Introduction 部分的构思方式。

The teacher leads the whole class to **discuss** what can be the thesis statement and write the purpose of this essay.

Each group fill in the form below to show how differently the two samples design the introduction part.

	Sample 1	Sample 2
Writing purpose		
Opening		
Thesis statement		
Predict what will possibly follow the thesis statement in the body		

Period 3

Step 1　Sharing and leading to the body part

The teacher invites each group to **share** their forms finished in period 2 in the Lan Mo app.

And students are asked to **choose** which one of the two thinking maps can best illustrate the structure of the body part of their guessing and **explain** why.

意图：教师通过图像化 Body 部分的一般结构，帮助学生进行概括和判断。

A.

B.

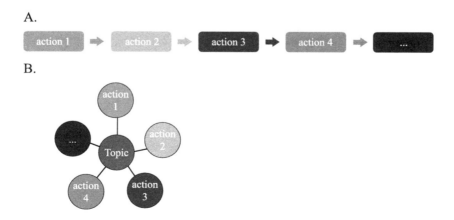

Step 2　Sample analysis

Students work in pairs and **visualize** the organization of Sample 5 on page 43—44, then **compare** in groups, and share in the Lan Mo app.

The teacher guides students to **search** for the key words in the textbook to **summarize** the main features of the organization of the body part of narrative essays.

(organized chronologically, flashback or flash-forward, transitional words/ time signals, verb tenses, temporal sequence)

意图：继续操练抓取关键信息的阅读策略，并通过案例5的图像化结构分析，帮助学生深入理解记叙文Body部分的结构特征。

Step 3　Conclusion part

Students **underline** the key words showing the connections between the introduction part and the conclusion part in Samples 7&8 on page 45—46.

The teacher guides them to **share** in class and **summarize** the function of the conclusion part: a restatement of the main point or to make a point to end the story, that is, to reflect the importance of the story narrated.

意图：学生通过案例分析和总结，操练抓取关键信息、选择性注意的阅读策略，同时增加对Conclusion部分的理解。

Period 4

Step 1　Revising the mind map

Each group works together to **revise** their mind map, adding points based on their own learning experience and what they've learnt in the textbook.

And adjective words will be added as judging standards like this:

意图：学生运用元认知策略修改原有的思维导图，综合课本知识和以往的学习经验，形成系统化的文体知识结构，掌握分析的要素及评价的常见标准。

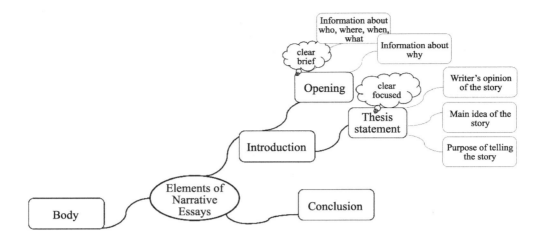

Students then **share** their maps in the Lan Mo app and then the teacher invites volunteers to **share**.

Step 2   Question–raising and comprehending genre knowledge further

Students **raise questions** in the Lan Mo app and then give "like" to the one they share similar doubts.
Students are invited to **share** their ideas to the top three popular questions in groups first and then to the whole class.

意图：学生运用元认知策略反思自己学习过程中的困惑，倾听同伴的想法，并在此基础上构建和分享自己的想法。

The teacher raises the question if students haven't mentioned this one:
What are the **differences** between narration and description?
Students can discuss with their group members and **thinking maps** are suggested to be used to explain their ideas.

意图：学生运用思维图将自己的表达结构化、图像化，并能区别描写与记叙的差别。

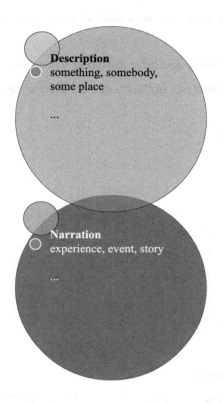

Description
something, somebody,
some place

...

Narration
experience, event, story

...

English Reading and Writing
Narrative Essays（2）— Reading for further comprehending

Targets: Freshmen majoring in English education

Preparatory course: Learning Strategies and Thinking Skills, Comprehensive English

Parallel courses: Comprehensive English

Prior learning: Descriptive Essays

Materials: Unit 3 Narrative Essays, *English Writing P46—55*, Shanghai Foreign Language Education Press, 2016

Teaching Philosophy: Think-oriented & mediation-based

Durations: 4 periods

Objectives: By the end of the session, students will be able

to **identify** introduction, body and conclusion parts and **summarize** the thesis statement/ main idea of the chosen narrative essays;

to **identify** time signals or other transitions and **sort out** the arrangement of supporting details;

to **identify** descriptions in the narrative essay and **infer** the writer's purpose;

to **select** key words and **visualize** their analysis of the chosen narrative essays to show their comprehension;

to critically **evaluate** the chosen essays.

Important/Difficult Point(s):

The analysis of narrative essays;

Critical evaluation;

Reflection on how they read a narrative essay.

Materials and Resources:

Courseware

Computer and projector

Procedure:

Period 1

Step 1   Reading for the thesis statement

The teacher asks students to read the title, the first and last paragraph of *My Present Wrapped in a Plastic Egg*, and **underline** the sentences indicating the main idea of this essay and circle the key words.

意图：引导学生应用文体知识，运用阅读策略归纳文章大意，理解题目和首尾段之间的关联。

Then the teacher leads students to **find out** what connects the title and these two paragraphs:

Ester day, present/ gift.

And then **summarizes** together the main idea of this essay:

Fourth egg hunt was the day I received most memorable gift, the gift of love.

Step 2　Reading for the body part

The teacher asks students to read the body part and use "□" to identify time signals and "■" to identify space signals and circle persons in the story. For example, Use "□" to identify "as", "■" to identify "around the front yard" and circle Gillion, Jason, my mother and I.

Students put the words of the places and people's names into the two squares below.

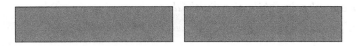

Students then need to **pick out** the verbs related to the persons and write them down in the **matching** columns below.

| Gillion | Jason | My mother | I |

Based on the key words and selected information above, students **discuss** in groups and draw a flow map of this story similar like this:

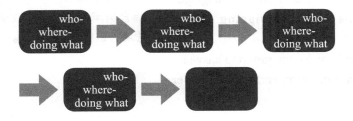

Each group can also **design** its own one by adding shapes or pictures.

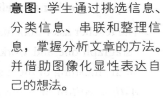

意图：学生通过挑选信息、分类信息、串联和整理信息，掌握分析文章的方法。并借助图像化显性表达自己的想法。

Period 2

Step 1   Teacher modelling—reading for description in narration

The teacher asks students to read the first three sentences of Paragraph one and works in pairs to draw a picture based on the meaning of these sentences.

With a yellow windbreaker on, Gillion looked like an Easter egg herself. Laughter filled our front yard while twenty-four plastic eggs dotted the lawn like a Seurat painting. The sun warmed our cheeks while the youthful laughter warmed out hearts.

意图：通过示范，引导学生整合新旧知识，加深对于描写的理解。

The teacher introduces this description in a narrative essay and asks students to **think about**:

What is the function and purpose of using description in the introduction part?

Step 2   Applying—reading for description in narration

Each group read the essay again and **compete** who can find more descriptions in this narrative essays. They **list** the key words and **explain** the function of using these descriptions.

意图：通过应用，帮助学生整合新旧知识，加深对于描写的理解。

Step 3   Question—raising for further analysis and critical evaluation

The teacher starts with the question:

Why does the author use present tense in the last paragraph? What do you think of this kind of designing for the conclusion?

And then the teacher randomly picks one group to answer.

This group will raise another question and invite another group to answer.

意图：通过对阅读内容的提问和回答串烧，引导学生综合运用文体知识，深入思考，进行批判性评价。

Period 3

Pair reading

Students need to work in pairs, read the two essays from page 53—55, and **visualize** their analysis.

Tips:

For the unknown words, in the beginning students just guess based on the context and then check after finish task 1;

Students follow the steps as the teacher has exemplified in period 2 and marks should be made in the textbook.

Students share their work in groups of 6 students and check whether they have picked out the same information and key words.

意图：通过合作阅读，进一步操练教师示范的阅读策略，在文章分析的实践中检查自身对于文体知识的理解度和语言方面存在的问题。

Period 4

Step 1   Question raising

Each group **discuss** about questions to each essay and **make a list**.

The whole class **share** questions in the Lan Mo app and if the questions haven't been mentioned in other groups, they get one star. Students show "like" in Lan Mo if they think that is a good question.

The group whose questions win most "like" gets one star.

And students **discuss** the answers.

意图：鼓励学生提问，同时引导学生批判性思考问题的质量。

Step 2   Essay evaluation

Each group of 3 students need to **design** a standard form and score each essay. After that, they write down **reasons** for the scores.

The teacher randomly invites one group to **share** their scores and comments, and other groups can add their opinions based on the precious group.

The teacher gives **comments** to their judgement in the end and makes a summary.

The form is suggested like this

意图：通过标准量表的设计，强化对文体知识的理解，并能够对所读文章进行有理有据的批判性评价。同时，通过反思任务完成的过程，进一步操练元认知策略的使用。

Standard form		Essay 1		Essay 2	
Writing Aspects	Detailed explanation	Score	Reasons	Score	Reasons
Writing purpose	Meaningful	5	...		
Introduction	Attractive opening				
	Clear and brief background information				
In total					

Students **reflect** the process on how they cooperate with their group members and what problems they have for the analysis and evaluation tasks, along with what they have learnt from the tasks and their classmates. They will **share** their ideas in the Lan Mo app.

English Reading and Writing
Narrative Essays (3) —Writing for applying and comprehending

Targets: Freshmen majoring in English education

Preparatory course: Learning Strategies and Thinking Skills, Comprehensive English

Parallel courses: Comprehensive English

Prior learning: Descriptive Essays

Materials: Unit 3 Narrative Essays, *English Writing* P51—52, Shanghai Foreign Language Education Press, 2016.

Teaching Philosophy: Think-oriented & mediation-based

Durations: 4 periods

Objectives: By the end of the session, students will be able

to **plan** a narrative essay with strategies and visualize their thoughts;

to **arrange** writing contents with certain logic and consciously **adjust** the order;

to critically **evaluate** peer's writing and **provide** conductive suggestions;

to **revise** their own writing with clear directions and strategies.

Important/Difficult Point(s):

The planning of narrative essays;

Critical peer evaluation and feedback;

Essay revising.

Materials and Resources:

Courseware

Computer and projector

Procedure:

Period 1

Step 1   Topic setting

The teacher asks students to read the topics from page 51—52 and **circle** the words indicating the writer's attitude and the focus of the essay, like valuable, important, "first", funny/ embarrassing/ frightening…

Students **think about** their writing topic and fill in the blanks below:

An _____ experience with _____ (your family)

The teacher shows a relationship tree map about a popular TV series and explains that families always have conflicts and people start to doubt "What are families?".

意图：让学生通过思考标题，理解记叙文的主要目的在于记叙有意义的事件。同时，通过对"家人关系"这一争议性话题进行讨论，激发学生的表达欲望和对生活话题的深入思考，引用记叙的具体经历作为观点的论据，感受写作的意义。

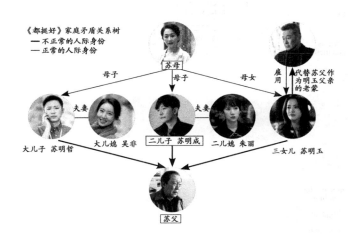

Discussing this philosophical question will be set as the task and students need to write the special experience with their family members to illustrate their ideas about "family".

Step 2　Planning for the introduction and conclusion parts

Students **make a list** about what information they need to collect for answering the question "what are families?"

意图：让学生在表达观点之前，学会收集信息，补充图式储备。

Each group of 3 students will share group members' lists and then divide the work to each one.

Students share what they have searched for the listed information in groups.

Then each group **discusses** their answers to the question.

Based on their ideas, each student **reflects** on their own experiences with their families, which can **illustrate** and support their opinions.

The teacher shows this graph to remind students of the essay structure and the main elements involved.

意图：通过图像化激活学生关于记叙文开篇和结尾的写作方式的图式，通过模仿和应用，进一步创造自己文章的收尾部分。

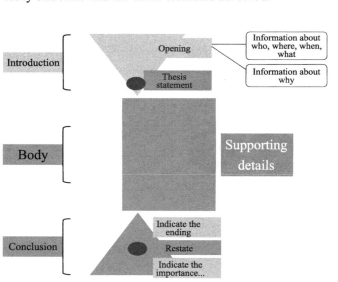

Based on the provided map, each student rereads the introduction and conclusion parts of the analyzing maps about the essays in the textbook again. They **design** how they start and end their essays, and then **visualize** their design.

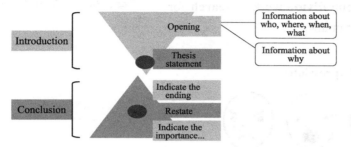

Period 2

Step 1　Planning for the body part

The teacher presents the thinking map below and suggests students to design the body part by adding time signals and space signals to show the changes of the actions from different persons.

意图：通过图像化激活学生关于记叙文正文部分的写作方式的图式，通过模仿和应用，进一步创造自己文章的主体部分。

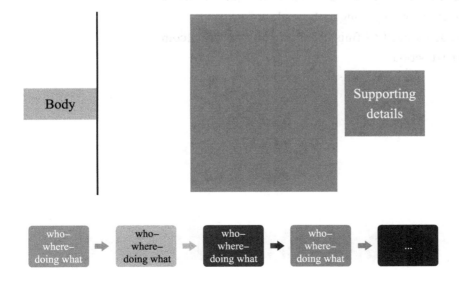

Step 2　Planning for the description part

The teacher presents four facial expressions indicating four types of feelings.

Students **discuss** what they can describe to strengthen the feelings of the readers and brainstorm in groups of 3 students. Then each group **divide** work to **search** for examples in the textbook or online.

意图：通过头脑风暴激活学生关于记叙文中的描写的作用的相关图式，通过收集、模仿和应用，进一步完善记叙文中描写部分的设计。

Facial Expressions

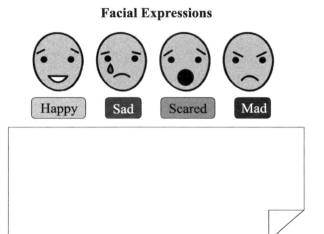

After that students **reflect** on their own design of their writing whether they can add some descriptions to make their essays more appealing to the readers.

P.S. Students need to finish their writing on Pigai.com before next period.

Period 3

Step 1　Lead–in for peer evaluation

Each group of 3 students **revise** and **prepare** their own evaluation standard forms.

The teacher introduces how students will work in pairs to evaluate peer's writing:

Fill in the information;

Visualize and **deconstruct** your peer's writing;

Compare your maps of analysis with your peer's planning map;

Ask questions if you have confusions about the content;

Score and give **reasons** and **comments** to your peer's writing;

Provide conductive **suggestions** onto their hardcopies.

意图：让学生了解同伴评价的步骤和目的。

Step 2　Peer evaluation

Each pair starts to work for peer evaluation. And then each writer will **discuss** the comments and suggestions with their peers.

意图：让学生实践，如何给予同伴批判性的评价和建设性的修改建议。

Period 4

Step 1　Group sharing

Each student **shares** in his group and 6 student in a group share their experience in 2 minutes by starting to say:

I think families are…

Taking my … and I for example.

Then each group needs to **vote** for the most convincing narration.

意图：让学生在组内分享，给予每个人表达的机会。

Step 2   Whole class inquiry

The teacher invites one group to **share** their most convincing narration and **explain** why.

Then the teacher says:

I agree with… Families are… But I want to add one more point. That is…

For example…

After the **demonstration**, the teacher invites other students who want to add points on this comment.

This map will demonstrate how the inquiry is going on among different students.

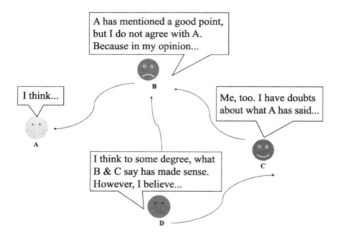

The teacher will give a **summary** to the inquiry.

Students **revise** their writing on Pigai.com after class and the teacher gives written **feedback** to them and interview 6 of them about their learning process next time.

Y 课程优质教学设计

第一部分
《中国文化概论》

一、课程价值

（一）课程性质与目的

《中国文化概论》是英语专业（师范）三年级的专业核心能力选修课。本课程以跨文化交际为着眼点，以中国本土代表性文化为主题，以英语语言为工具；通过本课程的学习，学生能够厘清中国文化发展基本路向，加深对中国文化内涵的理解，能使用英语准确、流畅地介绍中国文化，培养中国文化探究、传承和创新能力，提升中国文化对外传播推介能力。

（二）课程理念与思路

《中国文化概论》作为1+X+Y课程群中文化类课程代表，在1课程《英语学习策略与思维训练》、X基础语言类课程之后开设，通过目标构建、主题示范、文化探究三个模块，构建文化学习共同体以及对话式课堂，以体验式文化教学为指导，采用任务驱动、合作学习、问题解决等多种教学方法和手段，依托多种思维工具辅助，显性化学生思辨过程，提升学生文化内涵理解和表达能力；充分利用信息化现代技术和手段，依托社会文化资源（如图书馆、美术馆等），培养学生本土文化探究、传承与创新能力，提升学生资源策略使用能力。

（三）课程内容与任务

《中国文化概况》课程内容主要包括中国文化概览、哲学宗教、文学、艺术、饮食、服饰、建筑七个主题，首尾分别辅以课程介绍和文化探究。课程介绍主要用于课程学习指导和学生需求调研，调研过程中主题可视学生需求进行调整，但概览与哲学宗教为必选主题；文化探究为课程学习总任务，学生分组依托社会文化资源开展小组合作文化探究、思辨和陈述。

章	教学内容	总学时	理论学时	实训学时
第一章	课程介绍	2	2	0
第二章	中国文化概览	2	2	0
第三章	哲学宗教	6	6	0
第四章	文学	4	4	0
第五章	艺术	4	4	0
第六章	饮食	4	4	0
第七章	服饰	2	2	0
第八章	建筑	2	2	0
第九章	文化探究	8	8	0
合计		34	34	0

二、教学案例

（一）设计理念

"中国宗教哲学"是《中国文化概论》的第一个主题，也是课程的核心主题。单元整体设计以图式理论和布鲁姆教育目标层级为指导，以三大宗教/哲学及其相互之间的联系为主线，通过"激活图式—新知输入—新知输出"三大主要学习环节，依托文化主题学习材料和体验式学习过程，实现语言能力、思维能力和文化内涵的同步发展，全程贯穿由低阶思维到高阶思维的进阶发展。

通过"中国宗教哲学"主题学习，学生能够了解三个宗教/哲学的核心理念（仁、义、空），能够利用现实生活中的例子进行解读与理解，能够在阅读三个相关典籍的基础上使用恰当的思维工具比较三者的异同。

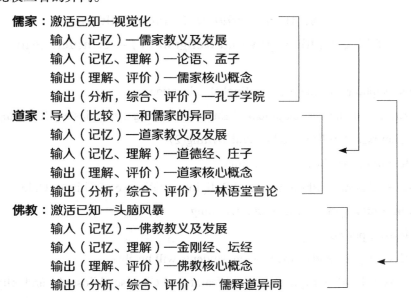

儒家：激活已知—视觉化
输入（记忆）—儒家教义及发展
输入（记忆、理解）—论语、孟子
输出（理解、评价）—儒家核心概念
输出（分析，综合、评价）—孔子学院

道家：导入（比较）—和儒家的异同
输入（记忆）—道家教义及发展
输入（记忆、理解）—道德经、庄子
输出（理解、评价）—道家核心概念
输出（分析，综合、评价）—林语堂言论

佛教：激活已知—头脑风暴
输入（记忆）—佛教教义及发展
输入（记忆、理解）—金刚经、坛经
输出（理解、评价）—佛教核心概念
输出（分析、综合、评价）— 儒释道异同

"中国宗教哲学"主题学时为六课时,覆盖核心的"儒、释、道"三大中国宗教哲学流派,主要学习内容和任务如下:

儒家:学生就"中国哲学宗教"主题以小组为单位进行自由绘画,激活并检测学生对该主题的背景知识,并通过小组陈述发现其知识缺陷;再通过匹配时间轴与主要宗教哲学流派的任务,细化学生对中国哲学宗教发展脉络的认识;针对教材上提出的中国宗教哲学特点引导学生进行批判;教师讲授儒家基本史实与核心概念,通过课堂提问的方式检测学生的理解情况,学生需要列举现实生活中的例子进行论述;学生就给定选段阅读分享学习心得,教师给予相应反馈。

道家:教师给出儒家和道家的主要特点,请学生分辨、归类,并加以说明,完成道家主题的导入与过渡,同时激活已知;其次,教师以工作表形式呈现《道德经》选段及其英文翻译,学生2人一组进行讨论匹配,强化对核心观点的认知以及相应的语言表达;教师讲授道家基本史实与核心概念,通过课堂提问的方式检测学生的理解情况,学生需要列举现实生活中的例子进行论述;学生就给定选段阅读分享学习心得,教师给予相应反馈。

佛教:教师讲授佛教基本史实及核心概念;学生阅读《金刚经》《坛经》选段并分享学习心得,教师进行即时反馈;教师引导学生分析佛教核心概念,学生就当代生活中的例子进行说明论证。

最后,学生小组讨论并填写"与众不同"图示(详见教案),并解释说明三大宗教哲学流派的异同之处,整体回顾本主题学习内容并进行分析、评价,教师给予适时点评。

(二)代表课例

An Introduction to Chinese Culture
Chinese Philosophy and Religion (1) —Confucianism

Targets: Sophomores majoring in English education

Preparatory course: Development of English Learning Strategies and Thinking Skills

Parallel courses: English Reading and Writing(2)

Prior learning: An Overview to China

Materials: Chapter 1 Philosophy and Religion, A Glimpse of Chinese Culture

Teaching Philosophy: Experiential Learning

Durations: 2 periods

Objectives: By the end of the session, students will be able

to **understand** and **critique** the typical features of Chinese philosophy and religion;

to **remember** the facts about Confucianism in China;

to **understand** the doctrine and spirit of Confucianism;

to **evaluate** the significance and effects of Confucianism in modern times.

Important/Difficult Point(s):

To understand the doctrine and spirit of Confucianism;

To evaluate the significance and effects of Confucianism in modern times.

Materials and Resources:

Courseware

Computer and projector

Procedure:

<u>Period 1</u>

Step 1　Visualizing the Chinese philosophy and religions

The teacher asks students to **visualize** the Chinese philosophy and religions in their minds to find out where they are.

意图：通过视觉化中国哲学和宗教，回顾并激活已知，引入本节课学习。

- Students **discuss** and then **draw** pictures of the Chinese philosophy and religions in groups; For example:

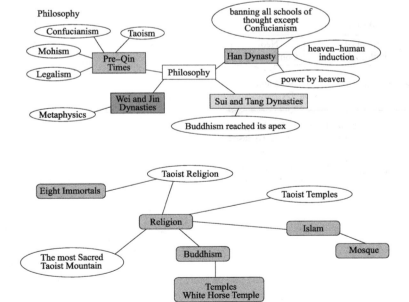

- Students then **compare** their paintings with other groups to see the differences;

- The teacher has a quick look around and choose some groups to present and **explain** their visualization in front of the class. The teacher then makes comments when necessary.

Step 2　Matching the Time Line of Chinese Philosophy

The question "How did the Chinese philosophy and religions develop then in the Chinese history" is asked, following the visualization. Students are given 2—3 minutes to talk to each other.

The teacher then presents a scrambled **timeline** for the development of the Chinese philosophy (see below). Students **match** the Chinese philosophy with its corresponding period. Questions are asked to help understanding while students are **making decisions** (e.g., "What are some of the typical features of Confucianism in the Han Dynasty? Any representatives?" "Why do you think so? Any evidences?") The teacher explains when necessary And answers questions from students if any.

意图：通过让学生填写对应时期的中国哲学主要流派，帮助学生回顾主要哲学发展脉络。

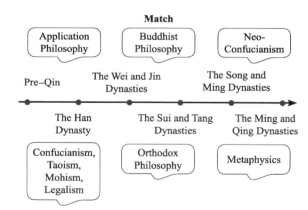

Step 3 Critiquing "Typical Features" of the Chinese philosophy

The teacher presents words of features of the Chinese philosophy to students with some letters covered and have students **guess** them and **justify** their choices. The teacher then reveals the covered words. Questions like "Do you agree?" "Anything you want to argue?" and "Can you give me an example?" are asked to facilitate understanding. Students will **critique** these typical features with necessary feedback from the teacher.

意图：通过让学生猜测遮住的单词让学生参与课堂，并通过批判教材给出的特征加深了解，评价中国哲学宗教的主要特点。

The **Basic features** of Ancient Chinese Philosophy

- Spiritual e_____e
- P_____e
- M_____y
- H_____y
- i_____n

Period 2

Step 1 Presentation

The teacher assigns readings of the history and key concepts to students before class (*i.e., Family of Confucius in Record of Historian* 《史记＊孔子世家》). In class students **present** key information and ideas with examples to the class and **answer** questions from their classmates. The teacher makes comments accordingly.

意图：教师课前布置学生阅读《史记＊孔子世家》，学生课上分组做主要信息呈现，学生记忆并通过举例加深对儒家精神的理解。

Step 2 A Jigsaw Reading of Excerpts

Students are given different excerpts from both *Analects* and *Mencius* (see below for some examples) to read for the meaning.

Excerpts:

知错能改，善莫大焉。《论语》

知之为知之，不知为不知，是知也。《论语》

意图：通过阅读原文加深对儒家精神的理解，通过信息差活动提高用英文表达中国文化的能力。

孟子见梁惠王，王曰："叟，不远千里而来，亦将有
以利吾国乎？"孟子对曰："王，何必曰利，亦有仁
义而已矣。王曰何以利吾国，大夫曰何以利吾家，
士庶人曰何以利吾身，上下交征利而国危矣。万乘
之国，弑其君者，必千乘之家；千乘之国，弑其君
者，必百乘之家。万取千焉，千取百焉，不为不多矣。
苟为后义而先利，不夺不餍。未有仁而遗其亲者也，
未有义而后其君者也。王亦曰仁义而已矣，何必曰
利！"《孟子》
孟子谓齐宣王曰："王之臣，有托其妻子于其友，而
之楚游者，比其反也，则冻馁其妻子，则如之何？"
王曰："弃之。"曰："士师不能治士，则如之何？"
王曰："已之。"曰："四境之内不治，则如之何？"
王顾左右而言他。《孟子》

In groups students **share** what they have read in English
and make **comments** as well on how this could be helpful
for their daily life.

An Introduction to Chinese Culture
Chinese Philosophy and Religion (2) —Taoism

Targets: Sophomores majoring in English education

Preparatory course: Development of English Learning Strategies and Thinking Skills

Parallel courses: English Reading and Writing (2)

Prior learning: Confucianism

Materials: Chapter 1 Philosophy and Religion, A Glimpse of the Chinese Culture

Teaching Philosophy: Experiential Learning

Durations: 2 periods

Objectives: By the end of the session, students will be able

to **remember** the facts about Taoism in China;

to **understand** the doctrine and spirit of Taoism;

to **evaluate** the significance and effects of Taoism upon the modern Chinese culture.

Important/Difficult Point(s):

To understand the doctrine and spirit of Taoism;

To evaluate the significance and effects of Taoism upon the modern Chinese culture;

To compare and evaluate the similarities and differences of Confucianism and Taoism.

Materials and Resources:

Courseware

Computer and projector

Handouts

Procedure:

Period 1

Step 1　Comparing Confucianism and Taoism

- Categorizing: Students in pairs are given opinions about both Confucianism and Taoism and are asked to put them under each **category** respectively (see below).

意图：通过对比儒家和道家，激活已知，巩固前面学习内容，并引入本节课学习，促进知识正向迁移。

Confucianism	Taoism
solemn social responsibilities	carefree flight from the respectability and conventional duties of society
human and mundane affairs	the transcendental world of spirit
a better relationship of human society	the nature for secrets of life
moralistic and commonsensical	mysticism and poetic vision

- Discussion: Students then **compare** their answers and explain their choices to each other. The teacher asks one pair to **present** their answer to the class. Where there is disagreement, the teacher asks follow-up questions for clarification and lead a discussion (e.g., "Can you define Tao in Taoism?" "What are some examples for 'people should follow the nature'?" "How is that different from Confucianism?") on students' understanding of Taoism and the way it **differs** from Confucianism.

意图：通过讨论加深对道家文化的理解，并发现知识不足之处，在后续教学中加以补充完善。

- The teacher introduces *Dao De Jing* as one of the classics of Taoism and asks questions on the basic information to check students' background knowledge (e.g., How many chapters are there in it? What does number 81 mean? Is Dao De one word or two words in Chinese?).

Step 2   Matching Chinse Lines in *Dao De Jing* with its English equivalents

The teacher then presents some chosen lines from *Dao De Jing* in both Chinese and English. Students **match** the Chinese original with its English equivalent (see below) and **share** their understanding with their peers.

意图: 通过匹配原文使学生接触道家的核心概念, 阅读原著并在合作学习中加深理解, 同时识记相应表达的语言形式。

道可道,非常道;名可名,非常名。	Tao never does; yet through it all things are done.
……大音希声,大象无形。道隐无名;夫唯道,善贷且成。	The Way that can be told of is not an Unvarying Way; The names that can be named are not unvarying names.
人之生也柔弱,其死也坚强。草木之生也柔弱,其死也枯槁。故曰坚强者死之徒,柔弱者生之徒。是以兵强则灭,木强则折。强大处下,柔弱处上。	There was something formless yet complete, that existed before heaven and earth;without sound, without substance, dependent on nothing, unchanging, all pervading, unfailing. One may think of it as the mother of all things under heaven. Its true name we do not know; "way" is the by-name that we give it. Were I forced to say to what class of things it belongs, I should call it Great. The ways of men are conditioned by those of earth. The ways of earth by those of heaven. The ways of heaven by those of Tao, and the ways of Tao by the Self-so.
为学日益,为道日损。损之又损,以至于无力,无为而无不为。	Great music has the faintest notes. The Great Form is without shape. So Tao is hidden and nameless, yet Tao alone supports all things and brings them to fulfillment.
道常无为而无不为。	Learning consists in adding to one's stock day by day; The practice of Tao consists in subtracting day by day, subtracting and yet again subtracting till one has reached in activity everything can be activated.
上善若水。水善利万物而不争,处众人之所恶,帮几于道。	When he is born, man is soft and weak; in death he becomes stiff and hard. The ten thousand creatures and all plants and trees while they are alive are supple and soft, but when they are dead they become brittle and dry. Truly, what is stiff and hard is a 'companion of death'; what is soft and weak is a 'companion of life'. Therefore, the weapon that is too hard will be broken, the tree that has the hardest wood will be cut down. Truly, the hard and mighty are cast down; the soft and weak set on high.
有物混成,先天地生。寂兮寥兮,独立而不改,周行而不殆,可以天地母。吾不知其名,字之曰道,强为之,名曰大。大曰逝,逝曰远,远曰反。	The highest good is like that of water. The goodness of water is that it benefits the ten thousand creatures; yet it self does not scramble, but is content with the places that all men disdain. It is this that makes water so near to the Way.

Step 3   Presentation (1)

The teacher has students **present** their summary of the history and key concepts (e.g., Dao, De, Non-action) of Taoism in the textbook. Students are expected to offer **examples** in their daily life to illustrate their points. Questions on understanding are asked to encourage a reflection.

意图：学生了解道家发展历史以及概念、内涵，通过应用概念分析当代生活来深化理解。

> Tao (Way): unchanging principles; the mother of all things; a way of harmony, integration, cooperation towards peace, prosperity and health;
> De: power of morality; adherence to Tao; the power of naturalness, of simplicity, even of weakness; It teaches of survival, of how to keep one's own integrity in the time of disorder
> Non-action: acting without artificiality, without overaction, without attachment to action itself; Do not allow outside things to entangle one's person, let events take their natural course, adopt an easy-going and unforceful manner

Period 2

Step 1   Presentation (2)

Students **explain** why Taoism is considered a religion besides philosophy and provide some basic information on it (see below).

(Taoism as a religion: Three Pure Gods-Jade Pure, Upper Pure, Great Pure; Religion of Five Dou of Rice; Eight immortals; Dragon-tiger mountain; a way of life according to the Way)

意图：帮助学生了解道家发展历史以及概念、内涵，通过应用概念分析当代生活来深化理解。

Step 2　Excerpt Reading

Students are given excerpts from Zhuangzi (see below) to read for meaning. They are expected to **explain** the relevance of the reading to the spirit of Taoism afterwards. For example:

惠子相梁，庄子往见之。或谓惠子曰："庄子来，欲代之相。"于是惠子恐，搜于国中，三日三夜。庄子往见之，曰："南方有鸟，其名为鹓雏，子知之乎？夫鹓雏，发于南海而飞于北海；非梧桐不止，非练实不食，非醴泉不饮。于是鸱得腐鼠，鹓雏过之，仰而视之曰：'吓！'今子欲以子之梁国而吓我邪？" ——《庄子　外篇》第六卷　秋水

意图：通过阅读原文加深对道家精神的理解。

Step 3　Revisiting Confucianism and Taoism

Again, the students are asked to work in pairs to **compare** Confucianism and Taoism with the aid of **Double Bubble Map** (see below) for the similarities and differences, and make thinking visible. The teacher chooses some pairs to **present** their findings, **compare**, and **discuss** with others.

意图：帮助学生记忆并再次梳理道家主要概念及理解内化。

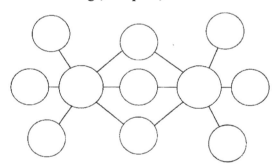

Step 4　Evaluation

Yutang Lin once claimed in his *My Country and My People* that "all Chinese men are Confucians when successful and Taoists when retired." The teacher asks students to **comment** on this saying and find examples in modern life to **argue** for or against it.

意图：学生通过运用前面所学概念对该句引文进行评价，深化对儒家和道家的理解，并区分其主要不同之处。

An Introduction to Chinese Culture
The Chinese Philosophy and Religion（3）—Buddhism

Targets: Sophomores majoring in English education

Preparatory course: Development of English Learning Strategies and Thinking Skills

Parallel courses: English Reading and Writing(2)

Prior learning: Confucianism and Taoism

Materials: Chapter 1 Philosophy and Religion, A Glimpse of the Chinese Culture

Teaching Philosophy: Experiential Learning

Durations: 2 periods

Objectives: By the end of the session, students will be able

to **remember** the facts about Buddhism;

to **understand** the doctrine and spirit of Buddhism;

to **compare** and **contrast** the similarities and differences of Confucianism, Taoism, and Buddhism.

Important/Difficult Point(s):

To understand the doctrine and spirit of Buddhism;

To analyze the similarities and differences of Confucianism, Taoism, and Buddhism.

Materials and Resources:

Courseware

Computer and projector

Handouts

Procedure:

Period 1

Step 1　Recapping of fundamentals in Buddhism

Before class students are asked to read the related chapter in the textbook as well as the assigned material. The class starts with a recapping by having students take a 5-minute quiz to recall some basic facts and ideas of Buddhism.

Quiz:

When did Buddhism first come into China?

What are the four noble truths about Buddhism?

Can you make a list of some key concepts of the Buddhism doctrine, e.g., transience?

What does the word "Samsara" mean?

Name some Buddhism classics.

意图：学生回忆对佛教的已有知识及概念。

Step 2　Dictogloss

The winner of the quiz will be given a short passage on Buddhism and reads it aloud 3 times in a normal speed to the class. The students make notes of the key words, and work in groups to **reconstruct** the passage. When it is done, some groups will **share** their passage with the rest of the class. The class works together to make a complete passage. The teacher then hands out the original copy for students to check up.

意图：学生通过听写活动加强对相关表达方式的记忆，以及运用已有佛教知识重构文本，加深理解记忆。

The passage:

The mind is a formless continuum that is a separate entity from the body. When the body disintegrates at death, the mind does not cease. Although our superficial conscious mind ceases, it does so by dissolving into a deeper level of consciousness. The continuum of our very subtle mind has no beginning and no end, and it is this mind that, when completely purified, transforms into the omniscient mind of a Buddha.

Every action we perform leaves an imprint, or potential, on our very subtle mind, and each karmic potential eventually gives rise to its own effect. Positive or virtuous actions sow the seeds of future happiness, and negative or non-virtuous actions sow the seeds of future suffering. This definite relationship between actions and their effects—virtue causing happiness and non-virtue causing suffering—is known as the "law of karma".

After we die our very subtle mind leaves our body and enters the intermediate state. In this subtle dream-like state we experience many different visions that arise from the karmic potentials that were activated at the time of our death. These visions may be pleasant or terrifying depending on the karma that ripens.

Step 3　Excerpt Interpreting

Students translate and **explain** the chosen lines taken from *Jin Gang Jing* and *Tan Jing* to their peers. They are encouraged to give **examples** for clarity and justification. They are also expected to find out what key doctrines are conveyed in them. For example:

一切有为法，如梦幻泡影，如露亦如电，应作如是观。《金刚经》

菩提本性，自来清净。但用此心，直了成佛。《坛经》

"须菩提，于意云何？可以身相见如来不？""不也，世尊。不可以身相得见如来。""何以故？""如来所说身相，即非身相。"佛告须菩提："凡所有相，皆是虚妄。若见诸相非相，即见如来。"《金刚经》

舍利子，色不异空，空不异色。色即是空，空即是色，受想行识，亦复如是。《般若波罗蜜多心经》

意图：通过阅读、翻译并解释原文，加深对佛教教义的理解，提高语言表达的流畅性与准确性。

Period 2

Step 1　Flash Writing

In turn students in a line **write** down key words for Confucianism, Buddhism and Taoism within 5 minutes without repetition. Then the last one of the line will write down all the words in the line on the black board. The teacher makes **comments** when necessary.

意图：通过速写儒、释、道的关键词，帮助学生回忆其主要概念和教义。

Step 2 Odd-One-Out

The teacher introduces the task "**Odd-One-Out**" and has students work in groups to **compare** and **contrast** Confucianism, Buddhism, and Taoism by filling in the worksheet (see below).

> Task setting up: The teacher introduces the rule of the task, and asks students to fill in the explosion shape with all the three philosophy shared, and the square with things shared by the two at the end and the bubble with things unique to the one;
>
> Modelling: The teacher models the task by offering words "world view" (for the explosion shape), "native religion" for square shared by Confucianism and Taoism, and "foreign" for the bubble of Buddhism.
>
> Task implementation: work in groups and fill out the shapes with key words. 1-3 groups are chosen to present and explain their work to the class.
>
> Task wrapping-up: The teacher makes comments based on students' presentation and gives lingual support when necessary.

意图：学生分析儒、释、道三家的异同，加深对三者主要教义及其相互联系的理解。

Odd-One-Out

第二部分
《英语课堂教学综合实践》

一、课程价值
（一）课程性质与目的

《英语课堂教学综合实践》是英语（师范）专业高年级开设的专业核心能力个性发展模块小学英语方向课程，是一门基于英语学科核心素养，将课程理念、课程改革与教学实践相结合的综合实践课程。通过本课程的学习，学生能够灵活运用所学外语教学基本理论、英语教学专业知识和思维工具对小学英语教学课例以批判的态度进行分析、评价，并将其运用于课堂教学实践；能够对英语语言知识和英语语言技能教学基本原则、活动设计和课堂实施有深入的了解和体验，并恰当地融入课堂实践之中，提升对小学英语课堂教学的敏感性，学会分析和处理英语课堂教学中的实际问题，提高英语课堂教学实践能力和反思能力，逐步形成规范、灵活、创新的教学实践能力。

（二）课程理念与思路

本课程实践性强，从课堂教学案例分析入手，帮助学生构建对英语语言与英语教学新的认识和理念，关注学生的学习过程、隐性学习策略发展与思维技能训练，有效培养学生发现问题、分析问题和解决问题的能力。教学方式采用案例教学法、项目学习法和任务型教学法，通过案例分析、项目制定和完成任务来学习，引导学生反思自己的教学设计和实施过程，引导学生去发现规律、归纳原则、分析评价，培养学生教学实践和教学反思能力。

本课程基于以学生为中心的原则采用"互动—参与—合作"的教学模式，即教学形式要求"互动式"，教学过程要求"参与式"，教学环境要求"合作式"，教学过程主要包括以下步骤：案例引入→分析点评→交流讨论→初步结论→活学活用→反思总结→创新改进。

（三）课程内容与任务

《英语课堂教学综合实践》课程内容主要包括英语语言知识教学实践、英语语言技能教学实践以及英语教学技能实践三个板块。英语语言知识教学实践涉及英语语音、词汇和语法；语言技能教学实践涉及听、说、读写四项基本技能；英语教学技能实践主要涉及英语故事与歌曲。教学实践任务要求学生运用外语教学基本理论和英语专业知识分析英语教学案例，掌握小学英语教学实践基本方法和技能，以小组为单位完成课堂教学实践并针对教学实践活动进行反思和改进。

二、教学案例

（一）设计理念

英语歌曲教学是小学英语教师应掌握的一种重要教学方法和职业技能。歌曲教学不仅能活跃课堂气氛、激发学习兴趣，还能培养语感，将语言知识和技能学习融入歌曲演唱之中，达到事半功倍的教学效果。通过本单元学习，学生应全面、正确了解歌曲在小学英语教学中的作用与目的，能够运用恰当方法与技巧设计、组织并实施英语歌曲教学。

本单元教学首先从学生学习经历入手，回顾并探讨歌曲的定义和特点，通过案例分析呈现英语歌曲的选择或改编原则与标准，以及歌曲教学的模式与步骤。在此基础上根据教学需要设计、实践英语歌曲教学，并在教师引导下开展互评、反思、总结、改进，提升英语歌曲教学实践能力。

本单元共计 8 个课时，主要学习内容与任务如下：

歌曲的意义与作用：教师邀请学生演唱并体验喜欢的英语歌曲，反思和总结歌曲的特点及歌曲在英语教学中的意义与作用。

英语歌曲选择与改编：学生通过体验英文儿歌，以小组为单位讨论并总结小学英语教学的歌曲特点和选择标准；各小组呈现分享英语歌曲选择标准，并通过同伴和教师反馈就英语教学中的歌曲选择标准达成一致意见；小组完善并制定基于教学需要的英语歌曲选择标准一览表；学生尝试运用制定的标准，基于不同教学主题选择或改编恰当的英语歌曲；学生分享并呈现所选择或改编的英语歌曲，同伴和教师提出建设性反馈意见；学生根据同伴和教师反馈对选择或改编的英语歌曲进行反思和改进。

英语歌曲教学设计：学生通过英语歌曲教学案例分析，归纳、总结英语歌曲教学步骤，尝试构建英语歌曲教学模式；师生共同探讨基于案例的英语歌曲"4 步教学法"；小组自选英语歌曲，并应用"4 步教学法"设计英语歌曲微格教学实践方案。

英语歌曲教学实践：学生以小组为单位开展英语歌曲教学实践；各小组对微格教学开展互评和教师点评，发现并指出英语歌曲教学实践中的优点和存在的不足，并提出改进建议；学生根据同伴和教师反馈意见改进英语歌曲教学实践方案，课后在微格实训室再次实践，并提交教学录像视频。

（二）代表课例

The Integrated Practice of English Classroom Teaching
Teaching of English Songs

Targets: Juniors majoring in English education

Preparatory courses: Development of English Learning Strategies and Thinking Skills, Mainstream English Teaching Methodology and English Teaching Reform, English Textbook Analysis and Lesson Planning

Teaching Philosophy: Case-based Teaching, TBLT

Durations: 8 periods

Objectives:

By the end of the lesson, students will be able

to **understand** the reasons and purposes for using songs, rhymes and chants in English teaching;

to **choose** and **adapt** English songs in English teaching;

to **analyze** and **identify** the teaching methods and modes for teaching English using songs;

to **design** and **try out** using songs, rhymes or chants effectively in English teaching;

to **evaluate**, **reflect** on and **improve** their using songs, rhymes and chants to teaching English.

Important/Difficult Point(s):

To design lessons based on English songs;

To practice using songs to teach English;

To evaluate, reflect and improve their teaching using English songs.

Materials and Resources:

Courseware

Children's English songs

Multimedia and OHP

Procedure:

<u>**Periods 1 & 2**</u>

Step 1   Ask the students to sing their favorite English songs and reflect on the singing process referring to the given questions.

- activate/calm down the students
- practice the target language (memorization)
- review what has been learnt
- develop language abilities (listening, speaking, reading and writing)
- create a relaxed classroom atmosphere
- interesting and relaxing
- to help memorization
- introduce a new language
- develop a natural sense of the language (the rhythmic nature, the interchange of stressed /unstressed syllables, the timing of stressed syllables)
- develop students' language knowledge (learning pronunciation, vocabulary, sentence patterns)

意图: 学生通过英语歌曲演唱体验，回顾并总结歌曲的特点及歌曲在英语教学中的作用与目的。

Reflection Sheet

1. What is a song?
2. How does the song help practise English?
3. What are you thinking about while you do the activity? The task of studying English, or something else?
4. Make a list of the reasons or purposes for using songs in English teaching. And share your ideas with the person next to you.

Step 2   Students experience sample English songs and discuss in groups the characteristics and the criteria of good English songs for primary English teaching.

- interesting and relaxing
- filled with fun and action elements
- demonstrate the rhythmic nature of the English language
- helpful to pick up chunks
- repeated key words and sentence patterns
- providing a natural context for language use

意图: 通过体验英语儿歌，讨论并总结用于小学英语教学歌曲的特点和选择标准。

- short in length, simple in vocabulary, vivid in content and easy to follow and remember
- close and familiar
- link to their life or experiences
- beautiful melody/strong rhythm

Step 3   Students present their criteria and decide on the criteria they agree upon.

意图：小组呈现、分享英语教学中的歌曲选择标准，通过同伴和老师反馈就英语教学中的歌曲选择标准达成一致。

Step 4   Students improve and make a checklist to sort out the criteria for choosing and adapting English songs.

Length: Is the length of the song/chant/rhyme appropriate for the students you are teaching?

Level: Is the song/chant/rhyme easy enough for the students you are teaching to sing/say? Remember they don't have to understand every word to enjoy the song, because they can pick up "chunks", but they will need to understand most of it.

Repetition: Is there any repetition of words, phrases or sentences? Repetition helps students remember the language and gain confidence in using it.

Content: Is it related to the language focus in the textbook you use? It may review things the children already know: it may also introduce a few words they will meet later in their English lessons.

Relevance: Is it related to the topic you are studying? Is it relevant to the children's interests and experiences?

Actions: Can your children do any actions when singing the song or saying the chant/rhyme? Actions help the students remember the words, underline the meaning, and make the song more fun.

Context: Does the song/chant/rhyme provide a meaningful context to help the children understand the language?

意图：小组完善并制定基于教学需要的英语歌曲选择标准一览表。

Catchiness: Does it have a tune or a rhythm that makes it fun to sing or say? Is it easy to remember?

Periods 3 & 4

Step 1　Students choose a topic and try to choose and adapt English songs for English teaching using the criteria made previously.

Students work in groups to choose and adapt sample English songs if necessary using the criteria made previously.

Topics: body parts, fruit, animals, colors.

Sample 1: Teddy Bear (An English song for teaching body parts)

Teddy Bear, Teddy Bear, Teddy Bear, touch your nose.

Teddy Bear, Teddy Bear, turn around.

Teddy Bear, Teddy Bear, touch your head.

Teddy Bear, Teddy Bear, touch your eyes.

Sample 2: If You Are Happy and You Know It

If you're happy and you know it, nod your head, (clap your hands/stamp your feet/say "ha" …)

If you're happy and you know it, nod your head.

If you're happy and you know it, and you really want to show it.

If you're happy and you show it, nod your head.

(angry, stamp your feet / hungry, touch your tummy)

Adapted/simplified one: *Are you happy? Can you show me? Clap your hands. Are you happy? Can you show me? Clap your hands. Are you happy? Can you show me? Are you happy? Can you show me? Are you happy? Can you show me? Clap your hands.*

意图：学生尝试应用先前制定的标准，基于不同教学主题选择或改编恰当的英语歌曲。

Step 2　Students present the songs they choose or adapt and give feedback to the chosen or adapted songs.

意图：学生分享、呈现所选择或改编的英语歌曲，同伴和老师提出建设性反馈意见，帮助学生正确认识在歌曲选择和改编方面存在的不足。

Step 3 **Students work in groups to improve their choice or adaptation of English songs for teaching one of the given topics.**

意图：学生根据同伴和教师反馈对所选择或改编的英语歌曲进一步完善改进。

Periods 5 & 6

Step 1 **Read and analyze the suggested teaching steps for *Old MacDonald Has a Farm*, and work out the mode of teaching English songs to primary students.**

Old MacDonald Has a Farm

Old MacDonald has a farm, E-I-E-I-O.
And on his farm he has a cow, E-I-E-I-O.
With a moo moo here and a moo moo there.
Here a moo, there a moo, everywhere a moo moo.
Old MacDonald has a farm, E-I-E-I-O.
Old MacDonald has a farm, E-I-E-I-O.
And on his farm he has a duck, E-I-E-I-O.
With a quack quack here and a quack quack there.
Here a quack, there a quack, everywhere a quack quack.
Old MacDonald has a farm, E-I-E-I-O.

Old MacDonald has a farm, E-I-E-I-O.
And on his farm he has a cat, E-I-E-I-O.
With a meow meow here and a meow meow there.
Here a meow, there a meow, everywhere a meow meow.
Old MacDonald has a farm, E-I-E-I-O.

Old MacDonald has a farm, E-I-E-I-O.
And on his farm he has some chickens, E-I-E-I-O.
With a chick chick here and a chick chick there.
Here a chick, there a chick, everywhere a chick chick.
Old MacDonald has a farm, E-I-E-I-O.

Suggested teaching steps for *Old MacDonald Has a Farm:*
Introduce the activity.

意图：通过英语歌曲教学案例分析帮助学生熟悉英语歌曲教学步骤，尝试构建英语歌曲教学模式。

Show children a picture of a farm and ask them if they have ever been to a farm and what they can see on a farm.

Show children a picture of a duck on a farm, talk to children about what a duck sounds like and how a duck walks. Ask them to imitate. Do the same with a picture of a cow.

Show a picture of Old MacDonald and tell children that he is a farmer and he has a farm. Tell children they are going to learn a song about the animals on his farm.

Narrate the song with actions, e.g. walking like a cat, opening and closing palms to indicate a duck's quacking.

Sing the song with actions.

Sing the song again and invite children to sing the E-I-E-I-O and the "quack" / "moo" part.

Sing the song again and invite children to sing along. (Do this twice.)

Ask children to sing the song with actions. Help them if necessary.

Divide children into groups to sing different parts of the song.

Get children to think of more animals and the sounds they make. Help with the names of the animals and the sound they make if necessary.

Get children to think of new verses for the song and sing their new verses.

Step 2   Students share their understanding of the teaching mode and the teacher gives feedback to present the mode.

The 4-stage mode of teaching English songs
Introduction: 1
Preparation: 2, 3, 4, 5
Relate the topic of the song to children's life experience.
Introduce to children the key vocabulary/structure in the song.

意图：师生共同探讨基于案例的英语歌曲"4 步教学法"。

Help children to understand the song with gestures.

Singing: 6, 7, 8, 9, 10

Let children listen to the song from the teacher or a tape.

Invite pupils to join in singing/saying and acting.

Let children sing the song on their own in chorus.

Let children sing/say different parts of the song

Follow up: 11, 12

Step 3　Students work in groups to choose an English song and plan their microteaching of the song using the 4-stage teaching mode.

意图: 小组自选英语歌曲，并应用"4步教学法"设计英语歌曲微格教学过程。

Periods 7 & 8

Step 1　Students are allowed 12 minutes for the micro-teaching and expected to do the following, while others act as learners and observers for the teaching.

Describe the learners (their age, language levels, and numbers of years learning English).

Explain why you chose this one. You can refer to the checklist of a good song, rhyme or chant identified earlier.

Identify the key vocabulary or structures/skills to be introduced or practiced.

Do the micro-teaching while others work as students and observers.

意图: 学生开展英语歌曲微格教学实践，其他同学扮演学生或观察者。观察者运用观课记录表教学过程主要信息。

Observation Sheet

1. What is the purpose for him/her to use songs, rhymes and chants in the teaching?
2. Do they help to achieve the purpose effectively?
3. How was the song, rhyme or chant introduced?
4. What did the teacher say when setting up and doing the activity?
5. Is there any problem in using songs, rhymes and chants in the particular teaching situation? And what solutions can you suggest?

Step 2   Students and the teacher give constructive feedback to the micro-teachings presented.

意图：对微格教学开展学生互评和教师点评，明确指出英语歌曲教学实践中的优点和存在的不足，并提出改进建议。

Step 3   Students go back to their respective groups to improve their micro-teaching plan and do it again after class by videoing it.

意图：学生根据同伴和教师反馈意见，改进英语歌曲微格教学方案并在课后在微格实训室再次实践，随后提交教学录像视频。

第三部分
《学术论文写作》

一、课程价值

（一）课程性质与目的

《学术论文写作》作为针对英语专业高年级学生开设的专业核心能力必修课程，主要培养学生创新性思维和学术研究意识，发现问题、分析问题和解决问题的能力，帮助学生顺利完成毕业论文写作。通过本课程的学习，学生能够熟悉学术研究的基础知识和基本概念，能掌握确定研究问题、查阅和分析文献、设计研究方案、收集和分析数据的基本程序和基本方法，能撰写符合基本学术规范的研究论文，为毕业论文工作顺利开展奠定基础；能在文献阅读和案例分析中养成批判性思维习惯，能运用主要的外语教育研究方法，设计教育研习方案，为在教育实习中顺利开展教育研习活动奠定基础；能在学术研究中形成学习研究共同体，共同参与确定研究问题、分析文献、设计研究方案等活动，开展交流分享和学习借鉴等学术活动，从而养成良好的团队协作意识。

（二）课程理念与思路

《学术论文写作》作为"学习策略与思维训练"双融入 1+X+Y 特色课程体系中 Y 课程——学术类课程的代表之一，在第 6 学期开设，帮助学生迁移《英语学习策略与思维训练》课程中所学学习策略、思维技能、思维工具等应用到学术阅读与写作中，基于人的学习行为模型、记忆系统、图式理论、思维可视化工具等基本理论，采用案例法、探究法等培养学生学术研究意识，重点发展学生分析、评价、创造等高阶思维，促进学生语言能力、学术能力和思维能力的同步提升。

（三）课程内容与任务

《学术论文写作》作为理论与实践并重的课程，共 5 章，其中第 1—3 章为理论章节，第 4—5 章为实践章节，详见下表。理论章节主要包括学术研究评价（质量、程序和类型）、学术研究基本概念（理论、假设、模型、变量、样本等）、学术研究过程（选题、文献综述、数据搜集与分析）、学术研究方法（调查研究、个案研究、实验研究和行动研究）等；实践章节主要包括学术论文题目、摘要、关键词、提纲、引言、结论、引用、参考文献等各部分的写作规范与写作实践。

《学术论文写作》学习内容与学时分配表

章节	教学内容	总学时	理论学时	实训学时
第一章	学术研究导论	4	4	0
第二章	学术研究过程	6	6	0
第三章	学术研究方法	8	8	0
第四章	论文写作实践	14	0	14
第五章	毕业论文要求	2	0	2
合计		34	18	16

二、教学案例

（一）设计理念

"学术研究方法"是《学术论文写作》的第三章，用时 8 学时。本章教学设计采用在线翻转教学"课前—课中—课后"三阶段学习任务形成完整的"自主学习—集体构建—答疑指导—检测反馈"任务链，教师以引导者的身份负责教学任务设计与调整、教学过程指导和监控以及教学效果检测与反馈；学生以学习者的身份参与学习活动，完成学习任务与检测、过程交流与讨论以及效果反思与反馈。

课前，学生自主学习外研社 U 讲堂视频资源，了解调查研究、个案研究、实验研究、行动研究等代表性研究方法；课中，在集体检测自学情况的基础上，学生分组对近年来在《中国外语教育》《中小学英语教学与研究》《中小学外语教学》等核心期刊发表的相关研究论文进行分析与评价，然后教师答疑和指导，再通过章节理论小测试和小结，帮助学生进一步熟悉和内化以上研究方法的基础知识；课后学生继续回顾与反思，在线反馈所学、所获和所惑，教师在线答疑指导，提升学生元认知能力和研究意识。整个过程通过课前自主学习任务，激发学生自我系统的打开，课中通过分析、评价、检测等任务保证学生认知系统的运作和已有知识的应用，课中和课后学生的思考、分享、反馈等保障元认知系统的持续运作。

（二）代表课例

Academic Paper Writing
Unit 4　Academic Research Methods

Targets: Juniors majoring in English education

Preparatory course: Development of English Learning Strategies and Thinking Skills

Parallel courses: Advanced English

Prior learning: Introduction to research, and research process

Materials: Self-compiled materials

Teaching Philosophy: Think-oriented & flipped learning

Durations: 8 periods

Objectives:

By the end of the session, students will be able

to **know about** the representative research methods;

to **understand** the basic writing criteria of research papers adopting different research methods;

to **analyze and evaluate** research papers adopting different research methods;

to **feedback** on what makes a good research paper adopting different research methods.

Important/Difficult Point(s):

Understanding of the basic writing criteria of research papers;

Analyzing and evaluating different research papers.

Materials and Resources:

Handouts

Videoed lessons

Courseware

Computer and projector

Procedure:

<u>**Periods 1 & 2**</u>

Pre-class:

Step 1　Introduction to survey research

- Students watch the videoed lesson, and **know about** the following:

  What is survey research?

  What makes a good survey research paper?

- Students **apply** the above and prepare for class **sharing**:

  Analysis and evaluation of the given survey research paper.

- Students **check** personal understanding of the above and prepare for class **sharing**:

  What makes a good survey research paper?

意图：学生通过课前微课导学，了解调查研究及调查研究类论文的基本规范，并通过"学以致用"和"理解自查"任务尝试应用所学理论知识，检测对所学理论知识的理解，为课堂分享与讨论做好准备。

While–class:

Step 1　Understanding and application: survey research

- Students **share** how they **apply and understand** survey research. The teacher facilitates to organize discussion, explains, and supplements relevant information.

  Students **analyze** and **evaluate** the given sample of survey research papers.

意图：通过学生微课任务分享和案例分析评价以及教师答疑补充点评，帮助学生共同检测和发现理论知识理解上存在的问题，构建对理论知识和概念的正确理解，并形成良好的合作学习意识。

Step 2　Questioning and quiz: survey research

- Students **raise questions** about what they doubt about survey research. The teacher facilitates to organize discussion, explains, and supplements relevant information.

- Students take part in the quiz about survey research. The teacher makes comments accordingly.

意图：通过学生提问、理论测试以及教师答疑讲评，帮助学生共同检测和发现理论知识理解上存在的问题，内化对理论知识和概念的正确理解，并形成良好的合作学习意识。

Post-class

Step 1   Summary and feedback

Students **summarize** what they have learned, thought, and argued for/against in the two periods and provide their **feedback**. Peers read and **comment** on the given feedback.

—What is survey research?

—What makes a good survey research paper?

意图：学生通过总结、反馈和互评所学所思所疑，调动元认知系统运作，应用元认知学习策略，最大化课程学习共同体价值。

Step 2   Introduction to case study

- Students watch the videoed lesson, and **know about** the following:

  What is case study?

  What makes a good case study paper?

- Students **apply** the above and prepare for class **sharing**:

  Analysis and evaluation of the given case study papers.

- Students **check** personal understanding of the above and prepare for class **sharing**:

  What makes a good case study paper?

意图：学生通过课前微课导学，了解个案研究及个案研究类论文的基本规范，并通过"学以致用"和"理解自查"任务尝试应用所学理论知识，检测对所学理论知识的理解，为课堂分享与讨论做好准备。

Periods 3 & 4

While-class:

Step 1   Understanding and application: case study

- Students **share** how they **apply and understand** case study. The teacher facilitates to organize discussion, explains, and supplements relevant information.

- Students **analyze** and **evaluate** the given sample of case study papers.

意图：通过学生微课任务分享和案例分析评价以及教师答疑补充点评，帮助学生共同检测和发现理论知识理解上存在的问题，构建对理论知识和概念的正确理解，并形成良好的合作学习意识。

Step 2   Questioning and quiz: case study

- Students **raise questions** about what they doubt about case study. The teacher facilitates to organize discussion, explains, and supplements relevant information.
- Students take part in the quiz about case study. The teacher makes comments accordingly.

意图：通过学生提问、理论测试以及教师答疑讲评，帮助学生共同检测和发现理论知识理解上存在的问题，内化对理论知识和概念的正确理解，并形成良好的合作学习意识。

Post-class

Step 1   Summary and feedback: case study

Students **summarize** what they have learned, thought, and argued for/against in the two periods and provide their **feedback**. Peers read and **comment** on the given feedback.

What is case study?

What makes a good case study paper?

How is case study different from survey research?

意图：学生通过总结、反馈和互评所学所思所疑，调动元认知系统运作，应用元认知学习策略，最大化课程学习共同体价值。

Step 2   Introduction to experimental research

- Students watch the videoed lesson, and **know about** the following:

  What is experimental research?

  What makes a good experimental research paper?

- Students **apply** the above and prepare for class **sharing**:
  Analysis and evaluation of the given experimental research papers.

- Students **check** personal understanding of the above and prepare for class **sharing**:

  What makes a good experimental research paper?

意图：学生通过课前微课导学，了解实验研究及实验研究类论文的基本规范，并通过"学以致用"和"理解自查"任务尝试应用所学理论知识，检测对所学理论知识的理解，为课堂分享与讨论做好准备。

Periods 5 & 6

While-class:

Step 1　Understanding and application: survey research vs. case study

Students **share** how they **apply and understand** the differences and similarities between survey research and case study. The teacher facilitates to organize discussion, explains, and supplements relevant information.

意图：通过学生分享和教师答疑补充点评，帮助学生共同检测和发现理论知识理解上存在的问题，构建对理论知识和概念的正确理解，自主迁移双气泡图思维可视化工具的应用，形成良好的合作学习意识和思维习惯。

Step 2　Understanding and application: experimental research

- Students **share** how they **apply and understand** experimental research. The teacher facilitates to organize discussion, explains, and supplements relevant information.
- Students **analyze** and **evaluate** the given sample of experimental research papers.

意图：通过学生微课任务分享和案例分析评价以及教师答疑补充点评，帮助学生共同检测和发现理论知识理解上存在的问题，构建对理论知识和概念的正确理解，并形成良好的合作学习意识。

Step 3　Questioning and quiz: experimental research

- Students **raise questions** about what they doubt about experimental research. The teacher facilitates to organize discussion, explains, and supplements relevant information.
- Students take part in the quiz about experimental research. The teacher makes comments accordingly.

意图：通过学生提问、理论测试以及教师答疑讲评，帮助学生共同检测和发现理论知识理解上存在的问题，内化对理论知识和概念的正确理解，并形成良好的合作学习意识。

Post-class

Step 1   Summary and feedback: experimental research

Students **summarize** what they have learned, thought, and argued for/against in the two periods and provide their **feedback**. Peers read and **comment** on the given feedback.

意图：学生通过总结、反馈和互评所学所思所疑，调动元认知系统运作，应用元认知学习策略，最大化课程学习共同体价值。

What is experimental research?

What makes a good experimental research paper?

How is research different from survey research and case study?

Step 2   Introduction to action research

- Students watch the videoed lesson, and **know about** the following:

  What is action research?

  What makes a good action research paper?

意图：学生通过课前微课导学，了解行动研究及行动研究类论文的基本规范，并通过"学以致用"和"理解自查"任务尝试应用所学理论知识，检测对所学理论知识的理解，为课堂分享与讨论做好准备。

- Students **apply** the above and prepare for class **sharing**:
  Analysis and evaluation of the given action research papers.
- Students **check** personal understanding of the above and prepare for class **sharing**:

  What makes a good action research paper?

  How is action research different from other research methods?

Periods 7 & 8

While-class:

Step 1   Understanding and application: experimental research vs, the other research methods

Students **share** how they **apply and understand** the differences and similarities between experimental research and the other research methods. The teacher facilitates to organize discussion, explains, and supplements relevant information.

意图：通过学生分享和教师答疑补充点评，帮助学生共同检测和发现理论知识理解上存在的问题，构建对理论知识和概念的正确理解，自主迁移双气泡图思维可视化工具的应用，形成良好的合作学习意识和思维习惯。

Step 2   Understanding and application: action research

- Students **share** how they **apply and understand** action research. The teacher facilitates to organize discussion, explains, and supplements relevant information.
- Students **analyze** and **evaluate** the given sample of action research papers.

意图：通过学生微课任务分享和案例分析评价以及教师答疑补充点评，帮助学生共同检测和发现理论知识理解上存在的问题，构建对理论知识和概念的正确理解，并形成良好的合作学习意识。

Step 3   Questioning and quiz: action research

- Students **raise questions** about what they doubt about action research. The teacher facilitates to organize discussion, explains, and supplements relevant information.
- Students take part in the quiz about action research. The teacher makes comments accordingly.

意图：通过学生提问、理论测试以及教师答疑讲评，帮助学生共同检测和发现理论知识理解上存在的问题，内化对理论知识和概念的正确理解，并形成良好的合作学习意识。

Step 4　Understanding and application: action research vs, the other research methods

Students **share** how they **apply and understand** the differences and similarities between action research and the other research methods. The teacher facilitates to organize discussion, explains, and supplements relevant information.

意图：通过学生分享和教师答疑补充点评，帮助学生共同检测和发现理论知识理解上存在的问题，构建对理论知识和概念的正确理解，自主迁移思维可视化工具的恰当组合运用，形成良好的合作学习意识和思维习惯。

Post-class

Step 1　Summary and feedback: action research

Students **summarize** what they have learned, thought, and argued for/against in the two periods and provide their **feedback**. Peers read and **comment** on the given feedback.

What is action research?

What makes a good action research paper?

意图：学生通过总结、反馈和互评所学所思所疑，调动元认知系统运作，应用元认知学习策略，最大化课程学习共同体价值。

Step 2　Further practice: critical reading of different research papers

Students try to **critically read more papers adopting different research methods** and be familiar with the criteria for papers using different researches.

意图：通过课后批判性阅读不同类型的学术论文，养成"学以致用"的良好学习习惯，为后续学术写作实践奠定基础。

参考文献 ▪

Anderson J R. The Architecture of Cognition[M]. Cambridge: Harvard University, 1983.

Bruner J S. A Cognitive Theory of Personality[J]. Psyccritiques, 1956, 1(12): 355–357.

Chamot, A. U., Barnhardt, S., El Dinary, P. B., et al. The learning strategies handbook. [M] NY: Addison Wesley Long–man (Pearson), 1999.

Dewey J. How we think: a restatement of the relation of reflective thinking to the educative process[J]. Journal of Hellenic Studies, 1933, 44(2): 223–253.

Flavell J H. Metacognition and cognitive monitoring[J]. American Psychologist, 1979, 34(10): 6–11.

Gagne R M. The conditions of learning.[M]. 3rd ed. New York: Holt, Rinehart and Winston, 1977.

Marzano, Robert J. Dimensions of thinking[M]. Virginia: Association for Supervision and Curriculum Development, 1988.

O'Malley J M, Chamot A U. Learning Strategies in Second Language Acquisition: Strategies used by second language learners[J]. 海外英语, 1990, 67(10X): 126–127.

Oxford R L. Use of language learning strategies: A synthesis of studies with implications for strategy training[J]. System, 1989, 17(2): 235–247.

Tishman S, Perkins D. The language of thinking[J]. Phi Delta Kappan, 1997, 78(5): 368–374.

Udall A J, Daniels J E. Creating the thoughtful classroom[M]. Texas: Zephyr Press, 1991.

Vygotsky L S. Thought and language[J]. Bulletin of the Orton Society, 1964, 14(1): 97–98.

Waters A. Thinking and language learning[J]. Elt Journal, 2006, 60(4): 319–327(9).

Weinstein C E, Mayer, R E. The teaching of learning strategies[J]. Innovation Abstracts, 1983, 5(32): 4.

Wharf B L. A linguistic consideration of thinking in primitive communities [M]. Cambridge: MIT Press, 1956.

陈钰. 英语演讲教学与大学生创新思维能力培养 [J]. 英语教师, 2016, 16(16): 29–31.

杜晓新. 元认知理论在思维训练中的应用 [J]. 外国中小学教育, 1993(1): 5–8.

谷振诣, 刘壮虎. 批判性思维教程 [M]. 北京: 北京大学出版社, 2006.

关文信, 张向葵, 刘秀丽. 学习策略与小学生思维能力培养 [J]. 中小学教师培训, 1998(4):16–18.

江丕权, 李越. 关于大学生的思维训练 [J]. 清华大学教育研究, 2004(4): 116–120.

柯莎拉, 仁德. 学习者策略: 教师指南 [M]. 北京: 人民教育出版社, 2007.

李荣华. 大学英语阅读与思维能力培养 [J]. 海外英语, 2014(14): 79–80.

刘伟, 郭海云. 批判性阅读教学模式实验研究 [J]. 外语界, 2006(3): 14–18.

潘亚玲 . 外语学习策略与方法 [M]. 北京：外语教学与研究出版社 , 2004.

宋航 . 非英语专业大学生英语学习中社会情感策略运用的调查研究 [D]. 武汉：华中科技大学 , 2007.

王帅 . 国外高阶思维及其教学方式 [J]. 上海教育科研 , 2011(9): 31–34.

王维利，陈元鲲，陈珊珊，等 . 评判性思维教学实践及效果评价 [J]. 中华护理杂志 , 2006, 41(9): 834–836.

文秋芳，王建卿，赵彩然，等 . 构建我国外语类大学生思辨能力量具的理论框架 [J]. 外语界 , 2009(1): 37–43.

文秋芳 . 中国外语类大学生思辨能力现状研究 [M]. 北京：外语教学与研究出版社 , 2012.

谢建伟 . 非英语专业学生大学英语写作课程中批判性思维能力培养 [J]. 考试周刊 , 2016(89): 81–82.

杨思贤，李子建 . 在课程与教学中发展学生的高阶思维———一项香港教研个案的启示 [J]. 课程教学研究 , 2013(3): 5–10.

游坤 . 提高高职护生评判性思维能力的教学研究 [J]. 广西医科大学学报 , 2007(1): 199–201.

袁炳宏 . 大学生 (非英语专业) 英语阅读元认知策略的性别差异 [D]. 上海：华东师范大学 , 2004.

张维友 . 英语学习策略与技巧教程 [M]. 重庆：重庆大学出版社 , 2004.

周绵绵，余笑，叶长彬 . 英语学习策略：English learning strategies[M]. 北京：科学出版社 , 2011.

朱智贤，林崇德 . 朱智贤全集：第五卷 思惟发展心理学 [M]. 北京：北京师范大学出版社 , 2002.